Magic Circles

A Lucky Duck Book

SECOND EDITION

Magic Circles

Self-Esteem for Everyone in Circle Time

Murray White

Los Angeles • London • New Delhi • Singapore • Washington DC

This edition first published 2009

First edition first published 1999, reprinted

SAGE Publications
1 Oliver's Yard
55 City Road
London EC1Y 1SP

SAGE Publications Inc.
2455 Teller Road
Thousand Oaks, California 91320

SAGE Publications India Pvt Ltd
B 1/I 1 Mohan Cooperative Industrial Area
Mathura Road, Post Bag 7
New Delhi 110 044

SAGE Publications Asia-Pacific Pte Ltd
33 Pekin Street #02-01
Far East Square
Singapore 048763

www.luckyduck.co.uk

Library of Congress Control Number 2008930270

British Library Cataloguing in Publication data

A catalogue record for this book is available from the
British Library

ISBN 978-1-4129-3535-7

Typeset by C&M Digitals (P) Ltd., Chennai, India
Printed in India at Replika Press Pvt. Ltd.
Printed on paper from sustainable resources

Contents

About the Author

Murray White represents the UK on the International Council for Self-Esteem, an organisation formed in 1990 and now established in over 70 countries. Its goals are to promote the concept of self-esteem and its significance in individuals and society and to facilitate the co-ordination of self-esteem activities and projects throughout the world. The most recent conference held in this country was in Liverpool in 2006. Speakers attended from North and South America, Australasia and Europe. Murray was a head teacher for 30 years. In 1990 the Institute of Social Inventions gave him the education award of the year for his pioneering work introducing Circle Time and said, 'it could be used with advantage in all schools'. His self-esteem programmes for the classroom received an enthusiastic response when he initiated the Supporting Children Learning Through an Understanding of Behaviour Project for the local education authority. He is recognised internationally as lecturer and consultant, having presented workshops and keynotes in Europe, the USA and all over the UK. His interactive presentations are designed to enhance self-esteem in many settings, including families, schools, organisations and for individuals.

His main studies in psychology, counselling and therapy were undertaken at the University of Surrey, the Psychosynthesis and Education Trust, London and The Parent Network, London.

Like many residents of Cambridge, Murray cycles everywhere in this wonderful city. He sometimes finds time to imbibe the cultural atmosphere and enjoys some quick games of table tennis with friends. He confesses that what are intended to be healthy brisk walks along the river usually end up as slow rambles. Details of Murray's work can be seen on his website: www.murraywhite-selfesteem.co.uk. He can be contacted at 5, Ferry Path, Cambridge CB4 1HB; esteemhere@aol.com

Murray White emerges as the earliest and most significant influence on the establishment of this group process in the UK. His contribution for practitioners of techniques to raise pupils' self-esteem and his inspirational work on Circle Time has helped to ensure that the emotional well-being of young people in schools is never forgotten. Through his work the lives of countless numbers of young people have been improved.

George Robinson and Barbara Maines,
Lucky Duck Publishing

Above all, watch with glittering eyes, the whole world around you – because the greatest secrets are always hidden in the most unlikely places. Those who don't believe in magic will never find it.

Roald Dahl, the final words of *The Minpins,* his
last book written for children

Acknowledgements

I owe much to John Heron, who was the Director of the Human Potential Research Project, and his colleagues at the University of Surrey for opening my eyes to the wonders of humanistic psychology and to Lady Diana Whitmore and her colleagues for giving me more inspiration during my studies at the Psychosynthesis and Education Trust, London. It was from the experiences I gained in these places that I was able to see what was needed on the school timetable and so Circle Times began. My thanks go to Robert Reasoner, President of the International Council for Self-Esteem, for the guidance I received in incorporating a clear self-esteem structure into the circles and to George Robinson, who, through his many superb Lucky Duck publications, has promoted the value of Circle Times far and wide. I must also include Christine Rees and Rachel Voss, two good friends and teachers who made some valuable suggestions about what they would like to see in this new edition. And, of course, I do not forget all the girls and boys and grown-ups who brought their magic to my Circles and to all those teachers and others who continue to do a Lighthouse. Thank you. You are great.

The 'diagram for behaviour change' principle on page 31 is the work of John Heron, author of *Helping the Client*.

The Quick Relax on page 137 is printed with the permission of B. Remsberg and A. Saunders, authors of *Help Your Child Cope with Stress*, Piatkus Books.

Please note: Where children are referred to in the text please substitute young people or adults if they are appropriate in your situation. Similarly with he and she. Both are used in the text.

Foreword

We first encounted Murray when we read an article in the *Times Educational Supplement* (*TES*) (30 May 1989) entitled 'Magic Circles'. Here was a primary head teacher describing the work he was doing to enhance self-esteem through a process he was calling 'Circle Time'.

We had just published our first pack on Self-Esteem and Positive Behaviour Management and were excited to be introduced to a new technique. Though we recognised some of the activities and games, we had never seen them presented within a cohesive practical package that recognised the children we worked with. One particular example he used in the article shone out for us because it so accurately described children with low self-esteem who, despite contrary evidence, found it hard to see the positive in themselves. An 11-year-old who is good at maths was doing a sentence completion exercise and said in a low voice, 'I'm good at maths' and then finished in a whisper 'sometimes'.

We were pleased to see Murray expand his ideas in 1991 to produce the first substantial book in the UK on Circle Time. With hindsight we think he made a mistake not to use Circle Time in the title. We kept in touch and were thrilled when he suggested he might publish with us at Lucky Duck. It was a great honour to have the 'father' of British Circle Time add to our growing list of Circle Time publications and in 1999 we published *Magic Circles*, reverting to his original *TES* article title.

With an association going back nearly 20 years it is still an honour to be asked to write the Foreword for this new edition. In fact, in looking at the structure and content, it is so different from the first edition and, with the addition of 'Picture This', it feels like a new book rather than a new edition. However, with all the new content, the essential elements that Murray conveys so well are still evident.

- The clarity of the process of Circle Time:

  'Circle Time is like the scaffolding which is erected to support a building while it is being built. It supports the children while they grow and develop their esteem. The teacher is the architect who plans and devises the activities and uses all her skill and experience to give information and assurances at the level the children need.'

- The aspects that are developed:

  Under the umbrella of self-esteem, within the security of the process, children develop a sense of security, identity, belonging, purpose, competence and well-being. Murray was writing these things years before Goleman (1995) introduced us to emotional intelligence or recent initiatives such as 'Healthy Schools', 'Every Child Matters' and 'SEAL'.

- Practical ideas:

  The book is full of ideas to implement immediately in the classroom. This is a practical book to pick up and use every day.

- A sense of hope:

  What bursts from every page is the same message of hope that inspired us in 1989. Here is a person who not only believes in young people but can inspire us to believe that we can make a difference. We can help every young person to believe they are important people, full of strengths and capabilities.

We hope you will find as much inspiration in this book as we have received from Murray over two decades.

George Robinson and Barbara Maines

Introduction to the First Edition

Probably the most important requirement for effective behaviour, central to the whole problem, is self-esteem.

Stanley Coopersmith, *The Antecedents of Self-Esteem*

Every teacher wishes for a class of pupils who all take pleasure in behaving well and are all keen to study. A room which contains such a class is a good place to be, an ideal learning environment. In order to achieve such a situation, the issue of self-esteem must be addressed as self-esteem is the pivotal point between success and failure in school. It has a marked effect on both behaviour and learning. The connection between behaviour and self-esteem is well documented; behavioural difficulties do not occur where a healthy level of self-esteem is present and research shows that the correlation between self-esteem and school achievement is as high as between IQ and school achievement. Where teachers are aware of, and adopt strategies which enhance, the self-esteem of their pupils, they find that attendance is high, that there is a real enthusiasm to learn and that relationships flourish. This book is a contribution to the understanding of self-esteem and sets out to show teachers and others responsible for the welfare of children and young people how they can help to enhance their self-esteem, while at the same time developing an awareness of their own. The ideas and strategies presented here are based on my experiences with children and on discussions with teachers and others in staffrooms and workshops over many years. I take this opportunity to express my appreciation to the many super young people and their mentors who shared such a lot of their lives with me.

Circle Times are now being conducted in schools and other settings all over the country for children of all ages. The teachers and leaders concerned need everyone's encouragement and thanks for the vital role they are taking in helping our children and young people attain the self-esteem they need to fulfil their potential and to lead productive, fulfilled lives.

Introduction to the Revised Edition

One sees clearly only with the heart. Anything essential is invisible to the eyes.

Antoine de Saint-Exupéry, *Le Petit Prince.*

The world of self-esteem and Circle Time has got much bigger in the UK since my article 'Magic Circles' was published in the *Times Educational Supplement* (*TES*) in 1989. Much much bigger. At the time there was a tremendous positive response to it from readers both here and abroad but it was not possible to foresee the long-term consequences. As it turned out the article and the book which followed acted like dropping a stone into a pond or planting a seed in the ground. The ripples have turned into waves and the saplings into a forest. Many teachers have adopted the idea and conducted their own circles and now, nearly 20 years later, Circle Time gets official recommendations in government literature and there is a proliferation of books about it. We have witnessed the passing of the Children's Act, Every Child Matters, the introduction of the Social and Emotional Aspects of Learning guidance, the Healthy Schools programme, the formation of the PSHE Association, and schools devote much time to philosophy, emotional literacy/intelligence, happiness lessons, and other activities which, in their different ways, all promote the self-esteem of their pupils. This is very good news, as the value of the possession of a healthy level of self-esteem cannot be underestimated.

The intentions in this new edition differ from the first and are fourfold. First it attempts to counteract the myths and misunderstandings about self-esteem which still abound today by setting out clear definitions given by leading authorities in their research on the subject. It is really important that the significance of the possession of a high, healthy level of self-esteem and the affect it has on both individuals and society is understood. It is very unfortunate to see the facts misinterpreted so frequently.

Second, to give some guidance on what individuals can do about having healthy self-esteem themselves. The good news is that we can always get ourselves more if we are prepared to invest the time and effort. Third, to advocate the wider use of Circle Time. Not only does this activity have a place in schools, both primary and secondary, but also in any establishment where a group of people is gathered. If the appropriate materials and activities are used I can see a genuine beneficial use for it from nurseries to care homes. The book is intended as a guide for those who wish to facilitate the promotion of self-esteem and personal development activities in groups of people of any age, from children in schools and After School clubs, to teenagers in Youth Clubs, students in teacher training and other colleges, members of Women's Institutes, Rotarians, business meetings, all places where people gather and where they could nourish and enhance their self-esteem by participating in Circle Times. The author has extensive personal experience of using this material in many different settings and the participants all testified to the benefit it brought them.

Fourth, to ensure that those who take responsibility for facilitating Circle Times have clear ideas on its structure and purpose, that they have addressed the issue of their inter-relating skills, and have taken account of all the preparations necessary to ensure a successful outcome.

Whenever I have received negative feedback about any Circle Time it has always been evident that this has been the reason. It has not been because of the process itself. Of course enthusiasm is to be commended, but first things first, so I hope if you are intending to be responsible for presenting Circle Times you will take account of the views and information in this book. I wish you much enjoyment and many rewards in your magic circles.

Existence never repeats itself. It is very creative and inventive. And it is good, otherwise, although Gautam Buddha is a beautiful man, if there are thousands of Gautam Buddhas around – if wherever you go you meet Gautam Buddha, in every restaurant! – you will become bored and easily tired. It will destroy the whole beauty of the man. It is good that existence never repeats. It only creates one of a kind, so it remains always rare. You are also one of a kind. You just have to blossom, to open your petals and release your fragrance.

Osho, *Beyond Psychology*, Discourse Five. Part of 44 discourses given in April and May 1986 on the many techniques of self discovery

1

Self-Esteem: What Exactly is It?

How it affects the lives of everyone and its significance for society

> I regard self-esteem as the single most powerful force in existence ... the way we feel about ourselves affects virtually every aspect of our existence ... work, love, sex, interpersonal relationships of every kind.
>
> Nathaniel Branden, *The Psychology of Self-Esteem*

If you stopped people in the street and asked if they know what it is that everyone has to some degree, which cannot be seen, but the amount they have can be identified by the words they speak and the actions they take, there would almost certainly be difficulty in naming it. Then when they were told the answer was self-esteem and challenged to define it there would again be difficulty. The majority would invariably say it is feeling good or being self-confident, although in a survey done by the Body Shop some time ago there were some very creative definitions, such as The Pursuit of Dreams, A Twinkle in the Eye and The Living of Life.

Self-esteem is certainly more than feeling good or being self-confident and is a complicated, absorbing subject to explain as there are so many views on it. Many people are interested in it and it provokes constant debate.

There are well over 1,000 research projects on self-esteem at the present time examining how it affects different aspects of our lives. The recently published book *Self-Esteem: Issues and Answers* (Kernis 2006) has 450 closely typed pages and 56 contributors and if you look on Google the number of entries under self-esteem is endless.

So here, to put you in the picture as simply as I can, my intention is to quote some of the most respected definitions of self-esteem. Reading them I am sure you will conclude that it really is an issue which is important in your life, because basically they all say if you have self-esteem life will be good and if you don't it will not be so good.

This quote expresses it much better than I can:

> High self-esteem is associated with high productivity, whether it is exemplified in academic achievement, creativity or leadership: low self-esteem is characteristic of the low achiever, non creative person and the follower.
>
> John Gilmore, 'The Productive Personality'

Nathaniel Branden, a great authority on the subject, makes the point very graphically when he writes that, just as we need oxygen for our physical survival, so we must have self-esteem for our mental well-being. Consequently it has a tremendous influence on how we lead our lives. We need to understand what it is and how to ensure that we have some of this precious commodity. Here are some definitions that I think explain it well:

Self-esteem

- is being at ease with the four aspects of the self: the physical self, the social self, the cognitive self, and the spiritual self

- is appreciating my own worth and importance, and having the character to be accountable for myself, and to act responsibly towards myself and others

> *Towards a State of Esteem*, the final report of the California Task Force to promote Self-Esteem and Personal and Social Responsibility, 1990

- is the sum of feelings about yourself, including the sense of self-respect and self-worth. These findings are based on two convictions: I am lovable and capable-IALAC

> Sidney Simon

Coopersmith was one of the first to research the meaning of self-esteem and he said it was

> The evaluation a person makes, and customarily maintains, of him or her self; that is, overall, self-esteem is an expression of approval or disapproval. Indicating the person believes himself or herself competent, successful, significant and worthy.

> Stanley Coopersmith,
> *Self-Esteem Inventories*, 1981

Branden's definition is widely regarded today as being the best. He expands on that and says

> Self-esteem is the experience of being able to cope with the basic challenges of life and of being worthy of happiness. It consists of two components: Self-efficacy-confidence in our ability to think, learn, choose and make appropriate decisions and Self-respect-confidence in our right to be happy, confidence that achievement, success, friendship, respect, love and fulfilment are appropriate for us.

> Nathaniel Branden, *The Six Pillars of Self-Esteem*

And Mruk agrees

> The lived status of one's competence at dealing with the challenges of life in a worthy way over time.

> Christopher Mruk,
> *Towards a Positive Psychology of Self-Esteem*

If you develop a high sense of esteem every decision you need to make and every challenge you face will be easier to deal with. A problem will be easier to solve, or if it cannot be solved then you will be able to handle it with greater poise and strength. The basic challenges of life include such fundamentals as being able to take independent care of ourselves in the world, being able to sustain relationships that more often than not are satisfying to oneself and the others involved, and having the resilience to bounce back from diversity and to persevere in one's aspirations.

Where did we get our self-esteem? How have we decided how much self-esteem we have, that is, whether we are of low value, high value or somewhere in between?

> Self-esteem is a set of unconscious self-beliefs, formed over a lifetime, reflecting our perceptions of our abilities, our lovability, and how we attribute causality for the events in our lives.
>
> John V. Shindler, *Creating a Psychology of Success in the Classroom*

Self-esteem is formed by the experiences we have from the beginning of our lives and our interpretation of them is reflected in all our behaviour. Do we feel in control of our lives or is it something to do with fate? Do we feel accepted or judged, criticised or empowered to attempt the actions we want to take? Do we have a sense of competence to achieve or a feeling of failure? If negativity rules, low self-esteem prevails. If the opposite is the case then we can be confident of this situation. The key question to ask is, 'Am I worthy and competent?'

Worth and competence are the twin pillars of self-esteem. For an in-depth explanation about how these translate into living your life, read Branden's books. In the next chapters you can find out how taking part in the circles will help you to discover them for yourself.

Like physical health, you can never have too much self-esteem. Where it is thought that some people do have excess of it, it is due to a complete misunderstanding and one of several myths which exist about the subject and which are constantly circulated and used by some for negative reasons. Boasting, bragging and arrogance are often thought of as associated with high self-esteem but are in fact a clear indication of the lack of it, usually brought about by a desire to overcome insecurity and a need to prove oneself to others. There is a compulsive desire to make comparisons and compete. Good self-esteem is not about feeling superior to others because you feel better than they are, or that you can do something faster or neater. Self-esteem is not conceit. Confusion about self-congratulation and narcissism is unfortunate: sound approaches to self-esteem are based on realism, not inflated self-images. If we examine the cause of the aggression of the bullies, and the problems of the other chronic misbehaviours – the fighters, the precocious and the children who are withdrawn or have adopted the life of a victim – we will realise that low self-esteem is at the root of it. These children are not being hostile to the system, which is how their actions are invariably interpreted, but behave as they do because of strong feelings of inadequacy and internal blame, a belief that they do not possess the ability or intelligence to succeed.

In fact, low self-esteem manifests itself in many harmful, unfortunate behaviours and causes untold turmoil and misery. Studies show that poor school achievement, truancy, crime, violence, alcohol and drug abuse, teenage pregnancy and suicide all have strong links to poor self-esteem. Dr Neil Smelser, co-author of *The Social Importance of Self-Esteem* reviewed over 30,000 studies and concluded that low self-esteem contributes to a range of behaviours that lie at the root of many social problems and believes that addressing this issue is the way these problems can be overcome.

When we talk of self-esteem we are thinking of our mental health as this quotation illustrates:

> One way of describing mental health is that it is the emotional resilience which enables us to enjoy life and to survive pain, disappointment and sadness. It is a positive sense of well-being and an underlying belief in our own and others' dignity and worth.
>
> Health Education Authority, 1996

The problem that *The Lancet* pointed out 20 years ago still seems in evidence. It said that doctors' surgeries were full of depressed people and that the nation was suffering from an epidemic of low self-esteem. In fact it has multiplied and seems to be affecting every area of life both in the young and old.

> Today's children are growing up too soon and the prospects for society and the world they will inherit look increasingly perilous.
>
> *Community Soundings*, interim report of
> The Primary Review, October 2007

Here are just a few of the studies on problems which are reported.

> The number of prescriptions given to children under the age of 16 for depression and other mental health diagnoses has quadrupled in a decade. GPs wrote more than 631,000 such prescriptions for children in the last financial year, compared to just 146,000 in the mid 1990s. Other figures suggest that the rate of anti-depressant prescriptions for the population as a whole has hit a record high. GPs consider the needs for antidepressants only after a careful assessment of the patient's clinical condition.
>
> Professor Magur Lakhami, Chair, Royal College of General
> Practitioners, *Openmind*, No.147, Sept/Oct 2007

Do you think these children feel lovable and capable or worthy and competent? There is now thought to be a causal association between early anxiety and future negative outcomes including depression and substance abuse. The organisation beat (the working name of the Eating Disorders Association) reports that eating disorders affect 1.1 million people in the UK, the majority being adolescent girls and young women. Obesity in the young is a national concern. We have the second-highest level of obesity in the developed world. At the launch of Improving Lives, Saving Lives, Dr Paul Cosford, Director of Public Health for the East of England, said in September 2007, that obesity needed to be a priority and that early intervention was needed, including as early as breastfeeding and weaning. Ofsted says that a quarter of 10–15-year-olds regularly get drunk and 5 per cent of 10–11-year-olds had been drunk at least once in the four weeks prior to being questioned. The Howard League for Penal Reform believes that 95 per cent of boys aged 10–14 get involved in some kind of crime. In 2007, 24,000 were admitted to hospital for self-harm using razors and glass burns, the youngest of whom was 9 years old. A national enquiry, 'Truth Hurts', claims that one in five girls between 15 and 17 have self-harmed. According to a survey of 1,078 children aged between 7 and 18 by the Anti-Bullying Alliance, one in three children are being bullied on the way to and from school.

Put these and the results of many other reports and surveys together and you can begin to see the extent of the problem. Callers to ChildLine have presented many different problems and have prompted the charity to warn of an 'alarming decline' in the mental health of children.

Fifty one per cent of the timetable and enormous sums of money are spent on initiatives to improve literacy and numeracy, yet the results are inconclusive. With children and young people displaying behaviour like this, maybe there is a missing X factor. Could that be self-esteem?

A small-scale investigation by members of the School of Education, University of Manchester, which reported some time ago, found that levels of self-esteem had decreased in the time children moved from Year 2 to Year 6 and that the scores of the 11-year-olds were considerably lower than those of the same age tested 13 years previously.

And for them to have a sufficient level of self-esteem, so they can move forward well in their lives, the grown-ups must take responsibility. But if the grown-ups do not have sufficient self-esteem themselves, they are not in a position to help. This sounds like a downward spiral and is what prompted David Law MP to ask in the Commons if 'society is on the brink'. It is said that one in four of the adult population suffers from some kind of mental distress.

> Mental health problems are now the biggest cause of absence from work, costing businesses millions of pounds a year in sick pay.
>
> Claire Harris, Cambridgeshire Primary
> Care Trust, October 2007

Other problems of behaviour that people are presenting are mentioned elsewhere.

> Apart from problems which are biological in origin, I cannot think of a single psychological difficulty, from anxiety to depression, to fear of intimacy or of success, to alcohol or drug abuse, to underachievement at school or at work, to spouse battering or child molestation, to severe sexual dysfunction or emotional immaturity, to suicide or crimes of violence – that is not traceable to poor self-esteem.
>
> Nathaniel Branden, *The Psychology of Self-Esteem*

I am sure that Branden is right. My 30 years as a head teacher and the experience of being with countless children in Circle Time and presenting self-esteem workshops for many adults convinced me that when low self-esteem is tackled and changes made, dramatic differences can happen. The facts given here illustrate what an enormous impact self-esteem has on the lives of individuals and the repercussions that has for society. The Self-Esteem Tree (p. 6) is here to show where the people contained in these figures are. Through the situations and conditions they have found themselves in they are not even beginning to climb the trunk. Yet it is possible for them to get all of life's assets on the branches and to reach the top of the tree. Healthy self-esteem is always available to obtain. It simply needs a signpost there to show them which way to go. For this to happen a concerted national campaign is needed at all levels including the government, the media, employers, unions, voluntary agencies, schools and universities to concentrate on this one issue using all the many options available. If done well, people would soon appreciate the changes, welcome the differences, a positive lifestyle would be the norm and society would be transformed in a generation.

If you wish to address your self-esteem, either for personal interest or because you are responsible for the self-esteem of others, then you can begin to test your awareness of it by looking at the activities listed in the next chapter. Later you can read how self-esteem is composed of several different components and when they are put together in a structured way by using various strategies and activities, will build a high authentic level of self-esteem.

A healthy level of self-esteem enhances your performance, increases your likelihood of success – is the rocket fuel of motivation and the bedrock of well-being and contentment.

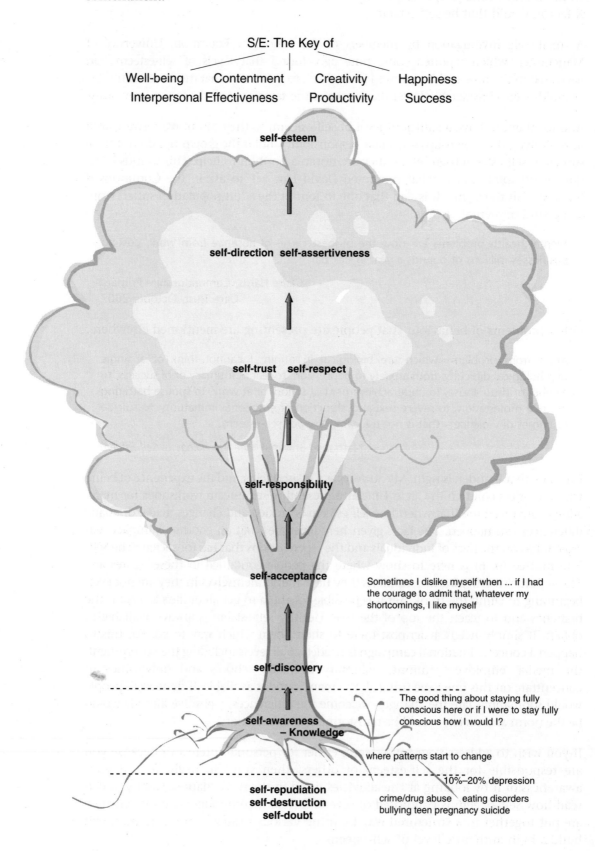

Your Self-Esteem

Your awareness of it and some steps towards nourishing it and enhancing it

	Known to self	Not known to self
Known to others	Open	Blind
Not known to others	Hidden	Unknown

Please look at this diagram (supposedly devised by two friends called Joseph Luft and Harry Ingram, (1995) The Johari Window).

- Self-disclosure opens the hidden area
- Feedback opens the blind area
- Experiment and play open the unknown area

1 Take time to list some circumstances and situations where you have opened your window, however slightly.

2 Self-esteem is based on openness and trust. Where have you been and who have you been with when you have:

- Disclosed things to others which weren't known before?
- Had information from others about how your behaviour appears to them?
- Discovered something new about yourself?
- What amount of risk do you think you took?
- Was there more trust between you and the others afterwards?
- Did your feelings towards yourself change in any way?

3 Discuss the answers with a friend.

Circle Time helps everyone to open their windows and to set their sights on new horizons.

Ever since I was born I have always seen myself as a lesser self.

Ivor Cutler, 1923–2006, Scottish poet, singer,
songwriter and storyteller

Ivor Cutler displayed his genius in his writings and appearances on radio, television and the stage over many years. Anyone who saw his retirement performance at the London Festival Hall would realise what a highly respected and much loved man he was. Yet at some stage he had revealed his true feelings about himself which showed he had been unable to cope with the key issue in his life. There are many others who appear extremely successful in their lives, who are well known and whose talents are acclaimed by all, but who choose to end their lives prematurely because of their opinion of themselves. Suicide is a national problem; it is the second highest cause of death among 16–25-year-old men.

Self-esteem

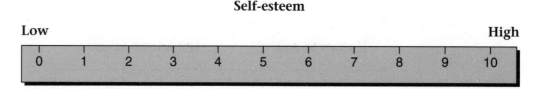

Your own self-esteem. On a continuum of zero to ten where would you put your self-esteem at the moment?

What does self-esteem do for you? How much do you have?

You should know that it is not a constant. It moves up and down a continuum according to the situation you are in and the position on it is dependent on your previous experiences. If, in life, you have had many positive experiences that enabled you to grow and build those qualities that encompass your self-esteem, then wherever you find yourself you will be more able to cope. If it is a challenging situation you will be able to draw on your self-esteem reserves. If negative experiences have left you with little or no reserves it would be much more difficult to deal with. If times are good you can bank some personal savings and have them to draw on if circumstances change. If you have no savings, then that is when problems arise. Many children today never leave the beginning of the self-esteem continuum. They grow up in circumstances where all they can do is just cling on to the end with their finger nails. These are the ones who, in order to survive, turn to alcohol, drugs, crime, and the other behaviour problems society is faced with. Parents with low self-esteem have little to give to their children and the downward spiral continues.

Awareness is the first step to change

Having a healthy level of self-esteem is a crucial investment in everyone's life. Awareness of behaviours and feelings is the first indication we have to discover how much self-esteem we possess. If you have not given a thought to your self-esteem before and how it is or is not sustaining you, here are some simple activities which you can do to test that awareness and to use as a guide to show what can be done to build and enhance your self-esteem.

Exercise A

Keep a journal for at least a week, making daily entries recording your experiences and using these statements. At the end of the time, note any changes that have occurred in your awareness or behaviour.

Today

- I learned that I ...

- I realised that I ...

- I noticed that I ...

- I discovered that I ...

- I was surprised that I ...

- I was pleased that I ...

- I was displeased that I ...

Exercise B

Give compliments.

1   If you are a teacher, give a genuine, thoughtful compliment to a student who concerns you every day for two or three weeks. It doesn't matter how brief it is. Do not be put off by any initial adverse reaction.

2   If you work with adults, give a compliment daily to a colleague, especially one who appears to need some extra support.

3   Give compliments to all those at home, friends, shopkeepers, all you come in contact with.

4   Be aware of your feelings when you receive a compliment. A compliment is enhanced tremendously by touch – from the gentlest touch on the arm or shoulder to the warm embrace. If words can't express it, say it with hugs.

If somebody listens, or stretches out a hand, or whispers words of encouragement, or attempts to understand, extraordinary things begin to happen.

Loretta Girzartis

Try these today!

I'm glad you're here (in this class/in this school/in this group)

I like the way you ...

(Continued)

(Continued)

I appreciate your help

That was great

I respect you for …

I really enjoyed doing that with you

That sounds a fine idea

I delight in your way of …

I celebrate who you are because ….

Exercise C

Take time to do this validation exercise with a friend or colleague. (How difficult it is, people say, but how worthwhile, they add.)

Partner A has three minutes to talk about all the things which make her good at her job. If she dries up, her partner, B, will say each time, 'Tell me more, please,' and at full time, for at least one minute, will give A a verbal pat on the back, e.g. 'It sounds to me as if you really do … well, and that you get a lot of satisfaction from it', etc. B generally shows appreciation for A.

B then takes a turn.

At the end, if you feel like it, give each other a hug.

Exercise D

Write the endings to these statements with the first thought that comes to mind. It may be best to do a few at a time to allow more time for reflection. Read them back slowly to yourself or discuss them with a trusted colleague. Did you discover anything?

- I'm happiest when …

- I feel saddest when …

- I feel most important when …

- I get angry when …

- A thought I keep having is …

- My friends are …

- I don't like people who …

- When someone tells me they like me I ...

- I appreciate ...

- I pretend to be ... when really I'm ...

- Something I do well is ...

- Something I'm getting better at is ...

- I have difficulty in dealing with ...

- I can help other people to ...

- Strong independent people... .

Exercise E

Ask yourself how you feel when you smile?

How often do you do it ?

Does it make any difference to the way you do your work?

Exercise F

1   Think of a time when you felt that someone wasn't listening to you. What did the other person do or say?

2   Think of a time when you felt that someone was listening to you. What did the other person do or say?

3   What conditions do you need in order to be able to listen?

4   What do you say, do or feel when you need to get the agreement of someone on an issue important to you?

5   Discuss the questions with a partner or in a triad.

Exercise G

1   Think of one or two people you admire, friends or ones in public life, living or dead. What qualities do they have which makes you admire them? Pick one of them which you believe you do not possess at all or you have but would like more of.

2   Consider which actions you would have to do for you to display this quality.

(Continued)

(Continued)

3   Meditate on it and visualise yourself using this quality when with others.

4   Tell a friend about it and ask if you can practise it in conversations with him.

5   In future, display this quality at every opportunity.

Exercise H

Choose a visualisation exercise from Chapter 8 or from the CD and repeat daily. Draw a picture and write about the experience.

Exercise I

By increasing your awareness of the emotions that others are feeling you will come to understand the emotions you have at certain times. Observation of how others react in situations will trigger how you behave in similar ones. Remember never to make a hasty judgement. These behaviours may be strong clues to a person's self-esteem but bear in mind an opinion should not be formed on one action or statement but on several over a period of time.

Security, identity, belonging, purpose and competence, these five senses are the building blocks of self-esteem.

A sense of security

Someone with a good sense of security

- feels safe enough to take limited risks and explore new ideas and places

- has a secure, strong relationship with a significant other

- is at ease and is comfortable with others

- is calm and centred

- can cope with change.

A person with a poor sense of security

- is unhappy with new experiences and situations

- is withdrawn and has little contact with people

- is looking for someone to trust and depend on

- is often fearful and worried and shows this by tics (spasmodic twitching) and habits, like biting nails, thumb-sucking and pulling at hair

- is seeking to establish safety by having clear limits and boundaries.

For you to do:

Listen to people talking and see if you can identify those with, and those without, a sense of security, for example, 'I like my work; the teachers are very kind and helpful', 'I don't understand what I'm supposed to do'. Watch how often people take risks. Observe their relationships with others.

A sense of identity

When a man no longer confuses himself with the definition that others have given him, he is at once universal and unique.

Alan Watts, *Psychotherapy East and West*

Someone who has a good sense of identity

- knows that others think he is special

- is imaginative, creative and able to express himself

- speaks positively about himself and others

- has a keen awareness of his own capabilities, attitudes and physical characteristics

- understands his feelings and how to deal with them.

A person with a poor sense of identity

- speaks negatively about himself and others

- is rarely imaginative or creative and finds communication difficult

- conforms to others' ideas and opinions and is dependent on adults

- may seek attention by misbehaving and will be undaunted by reprimands

- will be seeking to prove uniqueness, however negative.

For you to do:

Listen to people talking and see if you can identify those with, and those without, a sense of identity, for example, 'I've brought my collection of stamps to show you. I can't think of anything I like'. Do you detect any behaviour, e.g. conceit, which is masking low self-esteem?

A sense of belonging

To identify with and feel with another is marvelous ... those closely shared feelings are a special part of the bond between people.

Judith Brown, *I Only Want What's Best for You*

A person who has a good sense of belonging

- enjoys friendship, co-operates well

- communicates well and is comfortable with others

- knows that his opinions are listened to, and that he is wanted and liked

- is empathic, compassionate and sensitive.

Someone with a poor sense of belonging?

- is uncomfortable with others and will either withdraw and become a loner or will always demand attention

- communicates badly, either with reluctance or at inappropriate times

- relies on shyness or boasting to gain approval

- feels undervalued so will reject others and be insensitive to their needs

- is struggling, either through aggression or separation, to be appreciated and respected by others.

For you to do:

Listen to people talking and see if you can identify those with, and those without, a sense of belonging, for example, 'You can borrow ...'; a child will say 'There's never anyone to play with'.

A Sense of Purpose

Some mistakes are too much fun to only make once. Discuss this statement.

A person who has a good sense of purpose

- is self-motivated and will set goals for herself

- will try new ventures with enthusiasm

- has the determination to persevere and to succeed

- will ask for help and advice when appropriate

- accepts encouragement comfortably.

Someone with a poor sense of purpose

- will not risk the effort and possible failure

- sets impossible targets and unrealistic goals

- gives up quickly

- shows little initiative

- needs to be persuaded, cajoled, coerced.

For you to do:

Listen to people talking and see if you can identify those with, and those without, a sense of purpose, for example, 'I'm improving with practise'; 'Will you help me to get the equipment I need to do this?'; 'I don't want to do this'; 'Do I have to?'

A sense of competence

> The only way to succeed in life is to take off more than you can chew and then arrange with the mind to do it well.
>
> Kenny Everett on television, November 1991

A person who has a good sense of competence

- is able to make choices and take decisions

- will give support to others and is willing to share

- takes responsibility for her own actions

- can cope with setbacks and learn from them

- is able to acknowledge the strengths and accomplishments of herself and others.

Someone with a poor sense of competence

- needs constant external reward and has a helpless attitude

- is a poor loser and will blame others

- avoids responsibility and is reluctant to try new ventures

- is likely to be critical of any achievements of herself and others.

For you to do:

Listen to people talking and see if you can identify those with and those without a sense of competence: for example, 'I'm really proud of this model I've made'; 'I can see where I went wrong and shall not repeat it'; 'Why are things so hard?'; 'I didn't do it'.

Exercise J

Recall the assumptions you made when you saw some people for the first time. Think of people you like and know well. Remember the circumstances of your first meeting with them.

Who spoke first? What was said?

Exercise K

Remember a time when you were a child when you were happy.

Who was there?

What happened?

What other feelings were you experiencing?

Did you feel cared for and supported and have a strong sense of security?

If you are a teacher do you want the children in school to enjoy similar feelings?

Are you willing to spend time and effort finding out and putting into effect those practices which will achieve this?

If so, find colleagues who want to do this too and discuss ways you can work together

Exercise L

Write this sentence stem and give it six different endings:

If I had 5 per cent more self-esteem I ...

Exercise M

Write down a short-term goal.

What are the first concrete steps you could take to reach this goal?

Action? Place? Time? Are you going to take these steps?

What could keep you from reaching the goal, e.g., I don't want it badly enough, I'm afraid I might fail. What would it be like to succeed?

Write down feelings you would have if you achieved your goal.

Do it.

Use these exercises as a platform from which you can step to explore your self-esteem. In the resources section you will find a list of books which I believe are helpful if you wish to pursue an exploration of your own self-esteem and there are many websites which give information.

People who feel good about themselves produce good results.

S. Johnson and K. Blanchard,
The One Minute Manager

Facilitating Circle Times

Your responsibilities and the preparations required to lead a group well

What is facilitation and what exactly is the role of a facilitator? The dictionary spells it out. To facilitate: make easy, make possible, smooth the progress of, help, aid, assist. In Circle Times the job of the facilitator is to do all of those things primarily in order to empower and enable the others in the group to develop, to build, to enhance their self-esteem. That is obviously a responsibility, so I would say that before you take on that role and lead a group – irrespective of the ages of the members, whether young or old – thought needs to be given to what kind of qualifications and experience are needed. There are many different situations which will arise in Circle Times, so it is as well to consider beforehand how prepared you are to deal with them.

You will be the role model so you really should be in a good place yourself physically, mentally and spiritually. If we are responsible for others' lives as a teacher, parent or in any capacity then it is absolutely essential to be so. When you are seen to be behaving in the ways focused on in the group, the participants are much more inclined to understand and to try new skills. We should always be aware of the influence our self-esteem has on them. These are qualities which are desirable anyway but essential to have in Circle Times. If you are a teacher you will know that facilitating Circle Times is not something you do just by following instructions from a book. You need to demonstrate personal warmth by a good expressive vocabulary of feelings. Ask yourself if you are comfortable with emotional issues? Are you a good listener? Can you be a guide, not a judge, pointing out options without labelling them right or wrong, good or bad? Are you happy to lead without coercion, without taking credit, without being possessive and in a generous, nourishing manner? You might want to check out your sense of humour, your patience, your enthusiasm. You could make a list of qualities you see as essential for successful facilitation and see how many you feel comfortable with. Ask your friends to name the ones they see in you. Are there any that negate these?

If you need to or are keen to facilitate groups of any kind then get some experience of participation in groups that offer training in personal development and watch others facilitate. Choose ones where the reputation of the group leaders is acknowledged.

There are always a multitude of workshops and courses to choose from, from one-day ones to longer year-long ones. The latter are often offered part-time so that the sessions can be stretched over a longer period. Choose carefully as there is usually a big financial commitment to consider, but these are the ones where you gain the most. If you get the right one you will never regret the investment. The positive qualities you already have will be confirmed, you will explore and harness new ones and you will discover ways to overcome the ones which prove a hindrance in your life. When you have participated in the groups ask if you can be an assistant. Assistants do all the donkey work of preparing the room and clearing up etc., but it is an invaluable way to get close with a leader and pick up tips. Find out about the courses on websites and ask previous participants to give an opinion of their value.

You could also join a support group, or form one yourself, where there is a meeting of like-minded individuals where people want to set out the everyday issues they are dealing with and get opinions and support from others. If everyone has experience of group work it may well not need a leader, but make sure you feel it has a secure environment. It can consist of professionals who do the same work or totally different work. Often the perspective from the latter can be tremendously useful. To find time in a busy day these groups often meet first thing in the morning. Membership can be an excellent investment.

Here is a miscellany of practical tips. They will vary in relevance according to the Circle Time you are presenting:

- Be the first to arrive.

- Make sure the room is ready and that the furniture is where you want it to be. Be prepared to the smallest detail.

- Have all the equipment you are going to need readily at hand. If it's electrical, test it beforehand. Have handouts and worksheets in order.

- Greet each person briefly as they arrive. Remember their name.

- You are the model so must share first. Be open about your private life.

- Arrange introductions from the group and ask for reasons for attendance.

- Outline plans, make known where drinks are, toilet arrangements, etc.

- Draw up ground rules by agreement. Remember that it is crucial that all are made to feel safe and secure before proceeding. It needs to be made clear no judgement is going to take place and that there will be an encouragement to risk but no pressure to do so. If you make it clear that all have the right to pass you will find people will stop passing.

- Explain Johari Window and what is involved.

- Keep in contact by doing a Lighthouse, i.e. make eye contact round the group – frequently. Remain calm and collected but if you have some fear about being facilitator mention this authentically to the group.

- Be patient with irrelevant interruptions.

- Give clear instructions. Always check they are understood.

- Admit when you don't know the answer.

- Know when to insist you keep to agenda or let things wander.

- Be alert to the mixture of having fun or being serious.

- Give opportunities to jump about or sit still.

- Always integrate experiential activities. If you make comments about the process you will find the process works better.

- Watch the time, get the endings right.

- Be prompt restarting after breaks.

- Look after yourself.

- Throughout, always seek agreement for participation and give opportunities to question.

- Rule number one: remember Circle Times are experiential. The best learning takes place when there is a combination of seeing, hearing, saying AND doing.

The Theory of Self-Esteem and the Structure of Circle Times

The benefits that can be expected from participation by all ages

The Structure of Self-Esteem

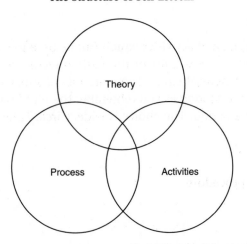

In order to understand what happens in Circle Time, think of three wheels. It is important to see how they interlock to get the full picture. The wheels represent the theory of self-esteem, the activities which enhance it, and the process which develops while it is happening. The first wheel contains the knowledge of how our self-esteem affects us and how we can use this information to be confident, motivated individuals and live a fulfilling life. The second wheel gives the details about the strategies and activities which can be used to implement the knowledge obtained in the first and in the third we see all the wheels turning together and the benefits which are the result.

The building blocks for a healthy future and a good life

The first wheel

There will certainly be a greater understanding of the processes involved in building self-esteem if you are aware of the components of it. Robert Reasoner, the highly regarded American educator and President of the International Council of Self-Esteem, now retired, has researched this area extensively and concluded that self-esteem is composed of five key building blocks. They are: Security, Identity, Belonging, Purpose and Competence. Reasoner tells us that having a sense of these five universally felt needs comprises the essential elements of self-esteem and that the whole process of enhancing it stems from an understanding of these feelings.

To have good self-esteem or to obtain it you need to feel:

- secure, safe and accepted in the environment

- special or unique and have a sense of your unique gifts. You may feel that only you do something in that particular way

- important and appreciated by people who you respect and whose opinion you value

- you are in charge and accomplishing things you set out to do. You feel you have a goal or a purpose and will be successful in reaching what you want

- that you have been successful or that you have made a difference. You have a feeling of self-pride and an attitude which says I can do it.

The second wheel

There are many strategies and activities which can be used in Circle Time to build the elements of self-esteem. Here is a list of the basic ingredients which, when blended together, will make a beneficial circle. There are lots of super self-esteem recipes you can put together yourself as long as you remember the building blocks and the whole diet is dealt with over a period. The choice is wide. Circle Time is never dull.

The ingredients include:

The 'Special Day' procedure

Rounds

Discussions and listening experiences

Games and energisers

Role play, movement and dance

Drawing, painting, art and craft

Touch-and-trust experiences

Relaxation and meditation techniques

Guided imagery and visualisation work

Journals, observation books, success diaries.

When the routines are established and the theory understood, teachers can diagnose elements that are lacking in individual children, and strategies can be devised and built into Circle Time which will help particular pupils.

The third wheel

If the theory is correct and the activities are successful, then the third wheel will turn and in the process the five universally felt needs will be growing in strength. The participants will come to enjoy and appreciate the secure environment which has been created, which is then followed by the practical steps offered to enhance their experience of the other four self-esteem building blocks.

Everyone needs time to think and learn

I emphasise that security is the pivot of the framework. When facilitating I never proceed in any circle, whether for children or adults, until I feel sure that it is firmly established. I say never, but I did once in the belief that the group had already done similar work elsewhere so I could proceed more quickly. It was a mistake. It does not matter how long it takes, people or children are not going to learn anything until they feel comfortable in the situation they are in.

We each learn in our own ways, by our own timeclocks

The second basic ingredient necessary for the growth of self-esteem is a sense of identity. In order to have self-esteem, each of us needs to feel special. We cannot afford to feel like a nonentity, like someone who does not matter. Both children and adults need to feel recognised as individuals and that they are worthwhile people whose ideas are valued by others. With this sense of identity will come a lot of self-knowledge, including an accurate description in terms of attributes and physical characteristics and a keen awareness of emotions and the part they play in life.

It's easy to make mistakes. That's the way we learn

As well as discovering their uniqueness, everyone needs a sense of belonging. We all need to feel needed and loved, and connected to other human beings. The way adolescents are influenced by their peers in their behaviour and dress is a powerful example, but the need remains with us throughout life and if we want to maintain a high level of self-esteem then we will make sure that we have a network of people who will satisfy that need.

It's intelligent to ask for help. That's the way we learn

Self-esteem also hinges on having a sense of purpose in life. When we develop one we will be motivated to set goals and will learn how to consider options and make choices. In a class Circle Time, the role of the adult at this stage is vital in order to ensure that the goals are realistic and achievable. A balance has to be arranged between security and risk and when it is attained success will generate more success. Adults get the same benefits when they attend Circle Time workshops of some kind. Their alternative is to seek help in counselling or life coaching.

We can do more and learn more when we are willing to take risks

Having a sense of purpose will in turn promote a sense of competence, which gives everyone the belief that they have the power to succeed in the things they regard as important and valuable. With this sense they will be aware of their strengths and proud of them. It is a delight for anyone when children experience success and express it as clearly as Christine, aged ten, did when she said to a student on practice, 'I'm really proud of my model. It's a nice feeling to feel proud, isn't it ?' Then you know they will be able to deal effectively and creatively with all life situations.

Discovering, exploring, enhancing the five building blocks of self-esteem enriches lives and helps everyone to:

- understand themselves, recognise their uniqueness, be able to express their own individuality and know that they have a special contribution to make to life

- initiate, develop and sustain mutually satisfying personal friendships

- be aware of feelings and handle them in a healthy way

- be able to handle upsets and conflict and resist peer pressure

- resolve problems into win–win situations

- deal with worry, anxiety and stress

- use and enjoy solitude

- like to co-operate and share

- excel at self-correction and self-direction.

Children, teenagers and adults will be more ready to welcome new challenges and the opportunities to take risks, they will be able to look for alternative solutions, make decisions and learn from mistakes, they will cope with any changes and difficulties and they will appreciate that life is a special occasion and they will rise to it!

> We can learn something new anytime we believe we can.
>
> Virginia Satir

The benefits for children, teenagers and schools

> The highest function of education is to bring about an integrated individual who is capable of dealing with life as a whole.
>
> J. Krishnamurti, 1895–1986, philosopher and educator

The list of benefits to personal self-esteem through participation in Circle Time is endless, but let me first deal with the objections, criticism and doubts about Circle Time.

Circle Time attracts much interest and from time to time negative remarks about it appear in the press and elsewhere and I would like to take this opportunity to challenge them.

The strangest must be a statement made by Dr Kathryn Ecclestone of Nottingham University. The *TES* quoted a remark allegedly made in her book which says that 'It's an approach which puts into pupils' heads the idea that all risk and excitement is bad and that any form of challenge is stressful'. You will know that this is the very antithesis of what it is about. It is very unfortunate indeed if any circle was actually seen which gave this impression. Others who may not have witnessed Circle Time in action may believe this nonsense and perpetuate it, so I was sorry that my offer to engage in public debate on the issue with Dr Ecclestone was declined. Circumstances prevail today which dictate that our attention to children's safety is critical. We must keep children safe but not overprotect to the extent that we stop them developing the skills and resilience to protect themselves. Circle Times are excellent vehicles where they can learn to do this.

There are any number of activities that can be used where, in a secure environment, they will discover how to make judgements on safe risks and be prepared to deal with danger. As for excitement, in my experience, and in the right circumstances, children love it.

> We need to ensure that 'safety first' does not drive out the opportunities children should have for experiment and development, and that our desire to defend young people against some very real dangers does not lead us into a sanitised world in which creativity and personal growth is stifled.
>
> Andrew Barnett, Director, Calouste Gulbenkian Foundation (UK)

The National Foundation for Educational Research in a 2004 report warned teachers that Circle Time might be fraught with pitfalls and cited as an example a difficult session when a child talked about a pet dying and this caused other children to cry. What is difficult about it? The child felt safe enough to want to divulge her grief to the group. Others cried sharing the pain. When something bad happens to children they often believe that they alone have experienced this situation. It is very cathartic for them to realise this is not so. Circle Time is an ideal forum for this to happen. Far better here than in the corner in the playground where it could turn into a form of hysteria. With a teacher's warmth and guidance the sadness is contained and everyone moves on. I can well imagine that the pet owner was then more able to concentrate on her day's work after that than if she had not made her feelings public. Adults cry at other people's grief so why not children too?

> Tears are as much about healing as they are about hurting.
>
> Julia Stokes, clinical psychologist, founder of Winston's Wish

Never try to avoid or ignore a trauma or just 'make allowances' for a pupil in crisis, as I am aware one teacher did when a boy's father died. It is on occasions such as this that the strength of holding regular circles in the classroom becomes abundantly clear. Bereaved children can benefit enormously by participating because it is at these times that support is needed, not just from the teacher but from peers as well. It is incredibly powerful when children feel safe enough to voice their worries and concerns and how liberating it is when their peers, along with their teacher, declare their support. I know of a situation in one school when a nine-year-old girl shared her concerns for the health of her mother, a single parent. The expressions of sincere care and practical backing that came spontaneously from all her peers moved the teacher to tell the rest of the staff that that experience alone would warrant holding Circle Times for the rest of her career. I think that an essential part of training for teaching should be a course in Reflective Listening, which would be a real asset for the newly qualified to have as they enter their classrooms for the first time.

If there is a really disturbed child in the group I presume that he will have been identified previously and be having special attention elsewhere. This is where the process known as Circle of Friends is so helpful. Circle Times will lessen the need for one-to-one exchanges with troubled children but there will always be some children who require this attention. See Moan Time in Chapter 8.

The children in the school where I introduced Circle Time had many personal difficulties in their lives. They were never expected or persuaded to talk about these but many welcomed the opportunity to do so. We never denied their feelings. We did not tell an angry child not to be angry, a frightened one not to be afraid or a child in pain to smile. Neither did we tell children they did not have a problem or say everyone has one. We listened and encouraged them to think of alternatives to the situations they faced so they could have the opportunity to get confidence in themselves. If there was no solution then as a staff our message to them was very clear: 'We are sorry, we cannot change things outside school but we are certainly going to support you while you are here'. It was always very obvious how much this was appreciated.

Confidentiality has been raised as a problem. I think it is only one if you want it to be one. Obviously the staff would never reveal anything unless abuse was evident and I am totally confident that the pupils did not take advantage of each other's life stories.

> Where children are anxious or distressed they need to believe that they attend a listening school and that the personal voice of individual children is valued and respected. For this to happen (from infants to top juniors and beyond) discussion needs to occupy a regular place in the school timetable. Contexts for speaking and listening need to be established within every classroom.
>
> BBC Education, *Teaching Today*

As Circle Time started promptly at 9 a.m. every morning – before registration – I have always concluded that that is the reason why punctuality was excellent and truancy non-existent. Of course Circle Time was offering a really good place to be with friends where they knew there would be no judgements, but it was also showing them ways in which they could cope better with what they faced and opening their eyes to alternative lifestyles.

You will be asking about those pupils who are seen to already have good self-esteem, be successful, well-balanced individuals. Can time spent in Circle Time be justified? No one can ever have too much self-esteem. Self-esteem always needs maintenance and can be further developed. It can be compared to physical health. No one can have too much. When we have good health it needs to be looked after and cherished. The same is true for our self-esteem. I have never seen a participant give any indication that time was being wasted.

Circle Time helps every child from the most able to the least able. It can happen that pupils with high academic ability will really benefit as it must not be assumed their ability makes them popular. They can feel isolated and different, and have to cope with being regarded as a freak or teacher's favourite. They often need time and patience to help them adjust socially or deal with antagonism from others.

The most common charge against Circle Time originated in America, where undoubtedly there was some justification, and then it translated into the columns of the *TES*, exposing some problems here. Some teachers were of the belief that the way to build self-esteem was simply to praise all the time, regardless of effort, trying to make pupils feel good at any cost. Of course if you do this it results in children having very odd ideas about their self-worth and seriously affecting their motivation and standard of work.

What was being overlooked was the need to address all the senses that enhance self-esteem. The creation of self-worth must be complemented by a similar emphasis on self-competence. Contrary to the flawed conclusions which get so much publicity, pupils with authentic self-esteem are well aware of the level of their abilities, do not accept insincere praise, will not back off from problems and are happy to face a new challenge with enthusiasm and confidence.

The only worthwhile praise is directed at the deed and not the doer and given in the form of feedback so that the child can see further steps to more progress, real competence and independence. Praise often but do it sincerely and reward genuine effort whenever you see it. Think of encouragement rather than praise. Again this is something teachers in training should know about before they leave college. It is so important because it has significant repercussions on pupils, in the way they judge themselves and their work.

> I am enough of an artist to draw freely upon my imagination. Imagination is more important than knowledge. Knowledge is limited. Imagination encircles the world.
>
> Albert Einstein

And finally there is a group of people, thankfully few in number, who apparently are totally unaware of what happens in learning of this kind, but still maintain it is a complete waste of time and continue to shout about it in the press. In an article in the *Sunday Times* (September 9, 2007) headed 'Happy Clappy Tosh', Chris Woodhead, ex-chief inspector for schools, wrote '"What did you learn in school today Johnny?" "How to be happy Mummy. I am proud of who I am." Children are happy when they are challenged by new knowledge, not when they sit around in a circle with their eyes shut'.

> You are trying to help people with long-term coping skills. I don't think there is a sane way to exist as a human being except to get in touch with your thoughts and feelings.
>
> Dr Anthony Seldon, Master of Wellington College

Space is now being increasingly planned on many school timetables for the promotion of the self-esteem of the pupils. The government is now actively encouraging it in secondary schools. Many other organisations are involved. Happiness lessons are now in vogue. Emotional literacy is a term frequently heard in the staffroom. Peer and adult mentoring is successfully happening everywhere, e.g. the National Black Boys Can Association. Educational kinesiology (brain gym) is very popular. Nurture groups are thriving.

The Howard League for Prison Reform is conducting conflict resolution workshops for 9–10-year-olds. Sex and relationships (SRE), drugs, anti-bullying programmes with various titles are being used in PSHE and citizenship lessons. They all have the aim in one way or another to promote self-esteem and well-being and that must be good for everyone. Of course, for strong mental health, physical development is essential too. An organisation called 'Food for the Brain' is running projects in schools with the aim of improving children's diet and nutritional awareness. The trials have produced a very positive impact on behaviour and learning.

> A skipping child is a happy child
> When you see a child skipping along the street
> you know that all is well in their world
> Why don't you see grown-ups skipping I wonder?
>
> Murray White

The whole school approach

The circle is the shape of harmony.

Twylah Nitsch, an elder of the Soneca tribe of North American Indians

Just as people see different things in a painting, a book or a film, when teachers discuss Circle Times in the staffroom or in workshops it often becomes apparent that they see different aspects of the process which they consider of value. However, whatever their age or experience, from student teachers to colleagues of long-standing, they all agree that Circle Times really do promote self-esteem in the community.

Circle Times do affect what happens in all the other exchanges which take place in the school day and hopefully their message does not conflict with all the other practices that go on in the institution. A practice which will benefit from the presence of Circle Times are School Councils, now operating in 95 per cent of schools. It will be the experience of activities, discussions and conclusions reached in Circle Times which will give the members of the councils the ability to make really meaningful contributions, but, even more important, they will attend meetings as true representatives of all the others in the school who have had opportunities to debate the agenda and come to democratic decisions in – and this is the key – self-esteeming environments.

A practice I had in school appears to have been updated by using computers now. Pupils send emails direct to staff asking questions, sending complaints, etc. I had a Why Box. This was a cardboard box which had been beautifully covered with material and had a big question mark sewn on each side. On the top was a slit, as in a voting box. It stood in the open library, a place where every pupil had easy access to it. Anyone could write a question of any type and put it in. Names on the paper were encouraged but not essential. Every Friday at the end of assembly it would be ceremonially opened and I had the responsibility of answering all questions in public, unless they were of an individual nature, in which case they were dealt with later privately. It was a delight because occasionally out would come a suggestion, something so simple yet so obviously beneficial to all that you could see the beaming smiles of the staff and hear the claps of the children.

Readers may also like to know of two other things I did which I thought were important and which paid dividends in the successful organisation of the school. On the notice board in my room was the word 'Yes'. I took it from one of those *Reader's Digest* adverts when you had to reply yes or no to the invitation to subscribe. My 'Yes' was there as an invitation to the staff. The message was, you are very welcome to approach me with your ideas. Can you suggest how the teaching, learning and the well-being of the children and staff who come into the building every day can be improved in some way?

Everyone knew that if it was feasible, time-wise and money-wise, then the answer was on the wall. We were able to do some wonderful things that came from these suggestions. I can tell you I never would have thought of them myself.

The second thing was always to start staff meetings with a round. The stem was only 'I...' and staff could say what they liked. People reported the good and the bad. They shared positive encounters they had had with pupils, they shared worries about organisation which were troubling them, anything which concerned them then and now. It was an investment in time I never regretted. Where the numbers of people attending allow this to be done, in school or anywhere else where people meet in a work capacity, do try it. Circle Time in action: it's about empowerment and that is about self-esteem.

> Children do not grow strong on their own. They need support from families, friends, schools and public services. They need opportunities to talk about their emotions with the people who influence their lives. They need structured activities to help them learn and grow. They need positive images, role models and positive aspirations.
>
> National Children's Homes Growing Strong campaign

It certainly pays dividends to examine all the nooks and crannies of the organisation to root out any practices which lessen self-esteem. How are the pupils told to enter the building, for example, or what happens at assembly or in the playground at lunch time? Research shows that it can take years off a child's life to overcome the bad effects caused by a low-functioning, negative teacher. The most casual remark which is a putdown is often remembered long after the rest of school is forgotten. Good support systems among the staff are crucial – everyone gains.

Useful questions to ask:

- Which present school practices are enhancing the self-esteem of the members of this community?

- Which present school practices negate the self-esteem of members of this community?

- What steps are needed to replace the negative practices with positive ones?

It is well worthwhile addressing these issues in any workplace, as well as in staffrooms, classroom Circle Times and School Councils.

> The relationships between child and child, child and adult, adult and adult are outstanding.
>
> Extract from HMI Report on a
> Cambridgeshire school

Learning to read – mini circles

It is a well-reported fact that when Paulo Freire went to South America in 1972 to start an adult illiteracy project he got nowhere until he realised how little people valued themselves and so he set up a self-esteem programme. Teachers coping with learning difficulties in children will not get the results they work so hard for until they deal with the self-esteem issues. If children doubt their ability to do something, no matter how good you tell them they are, then learning is difficult. Learning by rote has its drawbacks. They have to have the belief in themselves. In my time in school, for the children with the greatest problems, I used to arrange weekly small group sessions with the parents, the remedial reading specialist and myself. I would do my self-esteem bit (the parents' self-esteem!), then the reading help tips from the specialist and then the children would come and read a book with their parents.

I am not generally in favour of withdrawal groups. Studies show children do not like the exposure they feel but in this case it was bringing parent and teacher together which gave each child a combined message of loving and caring, two very important ingredients for growth. I think the children thought of these encounters as Me Time in a big way.

Children need

to feel acceptance and understanding before giving of their best

to feel secure

to ask questions

to learn how to cope with their fears

to feel good about themselves before they can learn from you

Cumbria Guidelines on Meeting Pupils' Special Learning Needs

Circle Time, targets, the National Curriculum, SATS, and league tables

Lord, when thou givest to thy servants to endeavour any great matter, grant us also to know that it is not the beginning, but the continuing of the same until it is thoroughly finished, which yieldeth true glory.

Sir Francis Drake at Plymouth

High self-esteem not only makes children – and adults – more responsible in their behaviour and more understanding towards others, but also brings alive qualities which give dividends in all other aspects of life, not least academic learning. To have a sense of purpose and a sense of competence manifests itself in vitality, enthusiasm, persistence and comprehension. High self-esteem is associated with high productivity and aspirations for excellent standards. Low self-esteem produces the opposite effect. This has quickly become apparent to those teachers conducting Circle Time with their classes. Here are some of the comments which have been made about it:

When I was first introduced to Circle Time about two years ago I was impressed by its almost immediate effect.

One of my early observations was how quickly the children's speech improved. One word became ten as they experimented with words and found a variety of ways in which they could be used.

There is stress on children being able to listen to each other, voice an opinion and sustain an argument. Circle Time is ideal for getting children into small groups to discuss issues and report back to the group as a whole.

Research by Purkey tells us that the correlation between self-esteem and school achievement is as high as that between IQ and school achievement. If the National Curriculum is going to succeed, children have to be able to communicate, decide, risk, be flexible, analyse, evaluate, and get along with others. It is no exaggeration to say that building self-esteem is the best preparation for success at school and in life.

In Circle Time children can take part as speakers and listeners with increased confidence and be actively encouraged to comment constructively. Ideas and information are re-evaluated and logical argument can be practised.

By giving the children something to talk about which they know, they become active participants in their own learning. They are able to see it is their thoughts and knowledge which are being valued and sought after, that they are a valuable resource.

I witnessed something special in a reception class in a school in Peterborough one day when the teacher excitedly pointed out a girl talking to two others in a simple game I had devised. She was happily taking her turn and really involved. It was near the end of her first term. The teacher told me it was the first time she had spoken to any other children. I have heard of this happening in other Circle Times. Of course where English is not the first language it is an excellent vehicle to encourage children to speak, as well as helping children of different cultures to mix freely. Statistics published in October 2007 revealed that one in seven children in primary schools do not have English as their first language and that 'white British' children are outnumbered in a fifth of local authority areas. Eye contact begins to come readily and the need to take turns becomes easily accepted. Language proficiency is a real strength of Circle Times.

Circle Time is about positive communication and interaction. The majority of the work is verbal. My experience with it has led me to believe that through this linguistically interactive process children will become better learners, because they develop greater confidence and ability through experience to understand the spoken word. It will also help them 'to express themselves effectively in a variety of speaking and listening activities matching style and response to audience and purpose' (National Curriculum English document: Attainment Target 1: Speaking and Listening).

Circle Time, behaviour and collaboration

The margins for behaviour change

1   Current limiting behaviour

2   Circle Time activities and skills training

3   Self-esteem and internal motivation

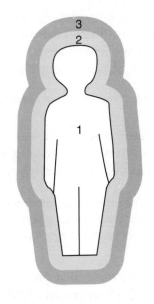

There is much that teachers can do to enhance children's self-esteem during the normal day-to-day casual exchanges which happen in every classroom, but they can never be enough. Important as these happenings are, time must be allocated when self-esteem is being actively promoted. Self-esteem really is as important as English and mathematics and needs a clear amount of time devoted to it on the timetable. It can be thought of as the fourth R – Reading, Riting, Rithmetic and Relationships. On that aspect alone, Circle Time merits the time devoted to it.

Its special strength is the effect it has on behaviour. Its value in training in human relations and interpersonal sensitivity is clear. Children learn to recognise how their emotions and actions are affected by others, and how the emotions and actions of others affect them.

They begin to learn new ways of looking at things, they are prepared to experiment with new behaviours and they have the opportunity to reflect on what these new experiences mean for them. All this can happen from a very early age. It can make a major contribution to developing and sustaining a high level of self-esteem.

A teacher who recognised the importance of these skills and how Circle Time would help wrote:

Circle Time has resulted in my being far less eager to sort organisation out in my classroom as I believe the children are quite capable of talking through and tackling these problems themselves.

This in turn gives them a greater sense of independence and responsibility. As they have more say in how the classroom is run they look after things better and take more pride in its appearance and running.

Another said:

I believe the children find Circle Time a valuable and meaningful part of the school day. They want to work harder and co-operate with others because they feel of worth themselves.

Wherever there is a human being there is an opportunity for kindness.

Seneca

Circle Time provides an ideal setting where collaborative learning methods can be tried and tested. Most children would prefer to work together as a group. Working together is a privilege and it is a rare child who wants to be left out for long. However, developing skills to work in a group is difficult; it does not happen by osmosis. It can be argued that learning to work together is as basic as learning to read and write and should therefore warrant the same amount of teaching time and effort. Statements by teachers who have conducted Circle Times include:

My comment is that Circle Time is a unifying influence in the class.

A later observation was about the way a collection of individuals with strong characters, not previously known for their empathy, was beginning to form into a cohesive and mutually supportive group.

When this group passed on to their next teacher I wondered what would happen, as their new teacher had a very different style to me. A month into the new term the teacher reported that the new class was wonderful and very together as a group.

A summary of a discussion on behaviour by a class of 10/11-year-old children

We talked about how we think other people see certain things that we do.

Some things were seen as weak, and some were seen as strong. (G stands for Good, B stands for Bad. Some things were seen as both Good and Bad.)

Strong		**Weak**	
Swearing	B	Moaning	B
Fighting in different ways	B	Getting cross	B
Telling	G/B	Hit and run	B
Walking away	G	Telling	G/B

Ignoring	G	Running away	B
Threatening	B	Chickening out	B
Calling names	B	Threatening	B
Crying	G/B	Calling names	B
Sticking together	G	Crying	G/B
Forgiving	G	Giving up	B
		Revenge	B

Here are the strong and good things we can aim at:

1   Walk away from trouble.

2   It's right to tell, sometimes.

3   Ignore provocation.

4   Stick together with your friends in good and bad times.

5   Forgive someone who's done something wrong to you.

6   It's good to cry sometimes.

Here are the weak and bad things we can try to miss: moaning, getting cross, hitting and running, telling tales, running away, chickening out of things, threatening people, calling names, giving up, taking revenge against someone.

Circle Time is not a cloning activity; it is about empowerment. The first step towards empowerment is awareness – becoming aware of why we are who we are and why we do what we do. Completion of the statements like those below is a very valuable process and children should be encouraged to complete them often, sometimes after a particular activity, sometimes to sum up a Circle Time itself. Obviously it will depend on the age and maturity of the children, but persistence of their use with even young children will soon bring rewards. The statements help them to evaluate and integrate their experiences, widening their horizons and increasing their awareness.

The list can usefully be on permanent display and the children can be reminded to use them on all sorts of occasions. If it is at all practical, arrange for the keeping of diaries or journals and have this list included frequently. It can become a very valuable record of a journey through Circle Time.

Today

• I learned that I …

• I realised that I …

• I noticed that I …

• I discovered that I …

• I was surprised that I …

- I was pleased that I ...

- I was displeased that I ...

Strategies which are discussed and learnt during Circle Times are then put into practice during other parts of the school day. If a self-esteem policy is to succeed, both parts are essential. It can be compared to a coin; obviously both sides are necessary to make it complete.

Where this has taken place, teachers have noticed 'A more pleasant atmosphere in the classroom', 'A unifying influence in the class' and 'much interactive, collaborative, and corroborative behaviour'.

One teacher wrote that

> after two years involvement with Circle Time, my school seems to be far more settled. There are far fewer instances of
>
> a) confrontations of an unpleasant nature between children
> b) children 'in trouble' standing outside the Head's office
> c) vandalism, aggression and complaints from parents and far more instances of
>   children showing responsibility for their actions
>   teachers emphasising the positive
>   co-operation and help from parents and children in the running of the school.
>
> This may be a huge coincidence ... but I think not.

When children are in a school where relationship skills are given time and attention, the impact on their lives is far reaching. Not only do these skills increase their immediate ability to communicate well, they give a real bonus in their adult lives. It used to be understood that social graces are learnt in the home but that can no longer be taken for granted, yet the ability to relate well to others is crucial for everyone.

The American National Labor Board conducted a large survey (1988) to find out why people got the sack. It discovered that the majority of employers were quite satisfied with the technical skills their employees brought to their jobs, but when they came in contact with others, whether it was the employers themselves, their peers, or, if the post required it, with the public, then they were less than satisfactory. Some 70 per cent of employees in the survey were dismissed for this reason. It would be interesting to have a similar study done in the UK today.

Circle Time and the home–school partnership

> A man who has been the indisputable favourite of his mother keeps for life the feeling of a conqueror.
>
> Sigmund Freud

Circle Time is an excellent device for drawing home/school interests together. I know of many instances where parents have noticed changes in behaviour in their children after participation in Circle Time and are naturally curious to find out what brought these about. Meetings called to explain the philosophy of Circle Time are usually well attended and received with enthusiasm. Parents quickly realise the value of giving their children a positive belief system and are usually eager for suggestions for activities which can be used at home. So, as well as promoting good relations between parents and teachers, it helps family relationships as well.

There are more instances of co-operation and help from parents now.

Parents are coming in to find out what is happening in the class to make their children so keen to get there.

Parents are asking for confirmation that the other children really did say those things about their child and are subsequently framing their Special Day certificates.

The truest test of civilisation is not the census, nor the site of cities, nor the crops, no, but the kind of man the country turns out.

Ralph Waldo Emerson

What the children think about Circle Time

In his school in ancient Greece, Socrates used to listen at doors. If he didn't hear laughter within five minutes he would enter the classroom to see what was wrong! Let's all use levity like yeast to lighten the necessary lessons.

Letter in *TES*, July 1991

It is when we are enjoying ourselves that we absorb the most. Smiles and laughter are powerful learning tools and bring real benefits to health as well. There are always plenty of both in Circle Time, and that makes even the serious issues that are dealt with easier to handle. It is a time which is universally popular with children. They are very perceptive about what is happening as these comments show:

Circle Time brings us together as a class.

I think it helps us to help, share and play with one another.

It gives us a chance to get geared into school work.

Circle Time is a good time because it is joyful and funny because you can say what you want and have votes.

I think Circle Time helps us not to be shy and worried.

It's a good way of letting the teacher know what you want and what your feelings are.

I think Special Days are good for us because it makes us want to come to school more and enjoy what we are learning at the same time.

Circle Time is very, very, very good.

Circle Time sets out to provide a setting where children will feel safe and supported and be secure enough to try out different ways of behaving – a real learning laboratory. It quickly finds favour with them. Of the hundreds of children that I know that have participated in Circle Time, apart from an initial reluctance from a very small number, they have all taken part with great enthusiasm. Their comments are witness to that, and, young as some of them are, they are able to express their opinions very well:

It gives you a chance to share your feelings.

You get to trust people more.

The clarity with which individual differences are accepted and valued are so appreciated:

It is very good in the way everyone gets a chance to speak and everyone listens to you.

I think it helps us as a class because everyone sees others' points of view.

It helps us not to be shy and to say what we think.

Being helped to grow emotionally and to enhance your self-esteem is a ver popular activity. Circle Time creates a climate where children can be truly spontaneous, and even though serious issues are dealt with, they will relax, sometimes laugh certainly learn and undoubtedly flourish. As one child wrote:

I realised there was nothing to be frightened of because we all shared each other's problems.

I hope you will agree that if I was in court as a lawyer defending the merits of conducting Circle Times in schools and called the participants as witnesses to ask them to give their opinions as evidence, I could simply say to the jury, as in the typical American film, 'I rest my case!'

Q. How can you delay milk turning sour?

A. Keep it in the cow.

A genuine response in 2006 GCSE exams

Compliments are good for you. To give is as beneficial as to receive

In *School Matters*, a survey of 50 London junior schools by Peter Mortimer et al., observers noted that teachers spent less than one per cent of their time giving praise. Another survey concluded that children hear about 15,000 negative statements in school per year. In a study of family life it was noted that the average child heard 16 negative statements for every positive one. Yet if children are to learn they need positive feedback 90 per cent of the time – we all do!

I believe that the first reason for the success of the Special Day procedure described in Chapter 6, is that the children know they will be appreciated and affirmed. I also believe, and there is evidence to this effect, that to help children gain high self-esteem, we need to positively teach them to give compliments to others and to get them to practise doing so. Unfortunately in many households compliments come low on the agenda and here we have a golden opportunity to correct a serious omission. This is why the Special Day procedure is such a powerful activity, a strong daily dose of self-esteem medicine to counteract all the negative statements in the environment.

I always caution teachers beginning Circle Time to expect to see change come slowly, but many notice differences in some children immediately and I'm sure it comes from taking part in this activity. It has even caused differences in parents' attitudes, as mentioned previously.

The Special Day theme was enthusiastically received by the children and as a result they kept asking for Circle Time. The children liked what they heard about themselves especially when a child with low self-esteem realised that others liked him and were prepared to say it with the rest of the class listening.

A rather difficult Year 1 child was described by the class when he was special as follows: he doesn't fight, he works hard, he helps us, all of which was blatantly untrue. However, for some considerable time after his Special Day, this is exactly how he behaved.

Seeing children participating in Circle Time made me realise how children can become self-confident. I would like to see Circle Time put into every junior and secondary school's daily schedule. If this could be implemented it would lead the less confident children into becoming whole adults with a true belief in themselves.

Keep self-esteem buzzing in your classroom

Verbal bullying among the pupils can cause so much unhappiness and it is important to counter the criticism and spiteful remark as strongly as possible whenever it occurs. I often used a plastic wand where the stars inside were held in suspension as my magic self-esteem thermometer. When there were put-downs in the room the stars would not show, as they were at the bottom of the wand. Nothing good was being said. This would provoke compliments as everyone wanted to see the stars moving, which of course was arranged by putting the wand behind my back and turning it upside down. It made a great visual reminder about what to say and what not to say to each other. Fun methods work best for young and old and you will find that even worldly wise teenagers appreciate messages given in this way.

There needs to be a common self-esteem vocabulary in use throughout the school. A name for positive statements needs to be chosen which will appeal to the children's imagination. The use of imaginative, colourful adjectives make a tremendous impact on promoting positivity in school. Then pupils will identify them easily and be reminded of their purpose.

I have no doubt whatever that the best way for pupils to understand the difference between a negative and a positive remark and the effect each has on the recipient is to hear their teachers read them *The Warm Fuzzy Tale* by Claude Steiner. They will quickly come to understand why warm fuzzies are so crucial and affirming to receive, while cold pricklies are so unkind to give and hateful and harmful to receive. The book was first published in 1970 and the concept of warm fuzzies and cold pricklies has since become a delightful symbol of the positive and negative strokes given and received in human living and loving all over the world.

Rather than adopt Steiner's vocabulary, you may wish to have an election and get candidates to propose words of their choice. The one with the most votes is adopted by all. Follow up with a campaign or slogan:

As important as fruit and vegetables

Everyone! Remember!

Five A Day: Give and Receive A Compliment – or more if you can

Ensure it appeals to the youngest and the oldest and then make sure everyone knows what it means. You can follow it up with mounting an exhibition of the ones which people liked best, with photographs of people giving and receiving them. It is necessary to remember that sometimes children never hear a compliment at home so need some guidance. 'Thank you', 'I appreciate that', 'That makes me feel good' on a list on the wall can be useful reminders.

A compliment is enhanced tremendously by touch – from the gentlest touch on the arm or shoulder to the warm embrace. There is conclusive proof that the immune system is enhanced by touch. If words can't express it, say it with hugs. If they are appropriate in your situation do encourage their use. Touch helps us to grow.

> A hug is the best gift you can give. It embraces all sizes and you can always exchange it.
>
> Kathleen Keating, *The Little Book of Hugs*

Try these compliments today!

- I'm glad you're here (in this class/house/workplace)

- I like the way you ...

- I appreciate your help

- That was great

- I respect you for ...

- I really enjoyed doing that with you

- That sounds a fine idea

- I delight in your way of ...

- I celebrate who you are because ...

Try compliments for the group, too.

Make statements which include everyone in the compliment:

- I really enjoy all your company.

- I think we all get on well together.

- I love it when I see so many smiles.

Stress in children and young people

The Education and Inspections Bill agreed in the House of Lords, November 2006, places a statutory requirement on schools to promote children's well-being as well as their academic achievement. In the Children Act 2004 the five goals of Every Child Matters are: be healthy, stay safe, enjoy and achieve, make a positive contribution and achieve economic well-being, viz. the promotion of: physical and mental health and emotional well-being; protection from harm and neglect; education, training and recreation; the contribution made by (a child); and social and economic well-being. Schools certainly have a challenge to achieve this. The authors of the Primary Review, Community Soundings, October 2007, report that 'we were frequently told that children were under intense pressure, and perhaps excessive pressure, from policy demands on the schools and the commercially driven values of the wider society.' Head teachers talked of SATs being 'demoralising' and 'destructive'. The pupils called them 'scary' and according to the Review, are losing their love of books in the drive to improve literacy levels. Of the primary school test results the report said:

> The rises exaggerated the changes in the pupils' attainment levels and were seriously misleading.

> We want to ensure that every child and young person has the self-esteem, resilience and social skills they need to succeed in life. We particularly want the most disadvantaged children and young people in the UK to have the inner strength to overcome the difficulties they face.

> National Children's Homes
> Growing Strong campaign

It was Abram Maslow, through his Hierarchy of Needs, who drew attention to the importance of a feeling of security in everyone's life. It was he who said, 'Only a child who feels safe dares to grow forward healthily. His safety needs must be gratified' (Maslow, 1968). Young people have a need for stability and structure. A sense of security indicates that they are grounded somewhere, yet today's figures tell us that one in five have an absent father. Many experience emotional deprivation when not brought up in a two-parent family. Research shows clear evidence of the adverse effects of this. Other difficulties many young children witness are the use of drugs, violence and crime and this strains security to its limits. Elsewhere at the same time we read that exclusions and truancy have reached record levels and that the number of children at Pupil Referral Units has gone from 7,000 to 15,000. Some of the latest figures given are that expulsions from secondary schools with 1,500 or more pupils have risen by 28 per cent since Labour came into power 10 years ago (*Independent*, April 2007) and that, 1,399,197 primary pupils, one in five, had truanted, a rise of 433,797 in 10 years in spite of government spending of £1 billion on the problem (*Independent*, October 2006). At interviews girls as young as 13 admit to getting purposely drunk every weekend and news reports tell us that binge drinking is the cause of a dramatic rise in liver disease. The link between these experiences is palpable.

A less obvious but major reason for stress in young people can come from the other end of the spectrum where in otherwise stable families the views and needs of children are not adequately taken into account. Then they will arrive at a feeling that they have no power in their lives, with little control over their days, always doing things according to someone else's timetable. Sometimes, in an effort to satisfy the unrealistic ambitions of parents, they will have a constant fear of failure, which will certainly induce stress.

Samantha Cartwright-Hatton, child psychologist at the University of Manchester, found that anxiety is possibly the most common disorder found in pre-adolescent children, and that the effects are not always short-lived; it can be a risk factor for the development of severe anxiety in later life. She also found that separation anxiety, which is the term used when a child feels stress when away from their parents/guardians, for example when in school, was the most common disorder found in children under 12.

Stress can make us both physically and mentally ill. Warning signals in children include inability to sleep, bad dreams, and listlessness, a previously sociable child becoming reclusive, or becoming aggressive in a way that is out of character. There has been a tremendous rise in children diagnosed with ADHD. Doctors say that there is an increased incidence of high blood pressure in children under seven.

Sir Michael Rutter, Professor of Child Psychiatry at the University of London, is quoted as saying 'For children in an unrewarding environment, good experiences at school can make quite a big difference. They can offer experiences which help certain children and are potentientially beneficial to all' (Robins and Rutter 1992). In view of the conclusions of the Primary Report, that statement is even more important today.

I maintain that Circle Time is an ideal forum to provide those good experiences and is the best way to introduce children to strategies to cope with stress to help in both the short- and long-term, dealing with immediate concerns and imparting a knowledge about how to deal with difficulties later in life. The anxieties about fear and conflict mentioned in the Primary Review all need to be addressed. We need to use everything in our armory to help children have a worry-free childhood. Circle Time is the obvious place to do this, a safe, non-judgemental environment where we can introduce every kind of strategy to achieve this.

Definition of Need

1   Physical care and protection

2   Affection and approval – gives identity

3   Discipline and control – age appropriate and consistent

4   Stimulation and teaching – input and learning

5   Opportunity and encouragement – gradually leading to autonomy

If any ONE of the five is missing the child will be damaged.

If any TWO are missing it will be difficult to achieve mature adulthood.

The Royal College of Psychiatrists, 1984

Visualisations

Physical fitness demands regular attention to exercise and diet. Mental well-being and a sense of self-esteem also justify time and effort. There is much of value in doing guided imagery with children. Apart from the sense of calmness which is achieved, they lead to increased self-confidence and self-acceptance and can do much to enhance self-esteem. As well as doing them in Circle Times, a good time to use them can be before creative writing and art lessons, or with an appropriate script where work is to be done in assessment conditions. Visualisations are also vastly superior to giving grim negative lectures about poor behaviour when the aim is to change attitudes and encourage a positive approach.

The use of guided imagery is good for adults too and has been found to be helpful in many ways. Studies suggest that it can directly affect the immune system. It can reduce stress, relieve pain, speed healing and help the body deal with a variety of illnesses from high blood pressure and heart disease to insomnia and depression. People who can visualise vividly, with powerful imagery and symbols, will gain most.

More details of the benefits that visualisations can bring and how to use them are given in Chapter 9.

The benefits for adults

Who says playtime is only for children?

Advert for ITV.com

I have been told that I am known as the Train Game man and with some justification, as I cannot remember ever doing a workshop when I have not included this activity. I do so because it enables a group of people who were probably unknown to each other at the start to go ssh-sshing like a steam train in a conga-like fashion round the room, all smiling, laughing and chatting to each other.

Ridiculous games like this encourage people to put aside any stress and anxiety they may have and enable them to deal with issues which will sustain them and help their personal growth. Adult men and women can still grow. Through professional facilitation the group will encourage maturity and what Maslow called 'self-actualisation'. If our levels of self-esteem have difficulty in coping with the negative feelings, thoughts and emotions that can accumulate as a result of our reactions to daily events and interactions, then a good way to stop and change is to seek out a group which uses these activities. By looking at the causes of low self-esteem and at what creates and enhances good, authentic self-esteem, people are encouraged to look at how their own level of self-esteem affects their lives. They will see what is relevant to them and examine their patterns of behaviour. Are they impeding self-fulfilment? Do the demons of negativity give 'not good enough' messages? Here in this supportive, relaxed, non-judgemental environment is the golden opportunity to see things from a new perspective and to discover new ways of expression. It's a time to get honest feedback from others. Circle Time gives us that special occasion to understand how others see us and find out how we get on with them. Where empathy is present it's a good bet that self-esteem will be nurtured and flourish.

You can see that many of the benefits listed in the previous sections obviously apply but there is one especially apt for this section summed up best in this quote

We do not stop playing because we grow old.

We grow old because we stop playing.

George Bernard Shaw

Studies have shown that laughter raises endorphin levels, which contribute to a feeling of well-being, and human growth hormone levels, which some say slows the ageing process. Also, experiments with volunteers at the University of Maryland School of Medicine in Baltimore, USA, found that laughing impacts how well blood vessels are able to expand. When a vessel expands it lowers the chance of heart attack and stroke. After watching a funny film researchers said that the increased blood flow in the volunteers was the equivalent of what would be seen after a 15–30 minute workout.

There is even another reason if you agree with Wittgenstein, the Cambridge philosopher, who is reported to have said that if you never do anything silly nothing sensible will ever get done!

Laughter is the music of the civilised world.

Peter Ustinov, playwright, actor, raconteur

In Circle Time we can be reminded of the advantages we can have in using our childlike qualities. In a long teaching career one of the best rewards I had was being encouraged to exploit mine by taking part in activities with many spontaneous, delightful children and young people.

So I am putting a reminder here about the good things which accrue from the Special Day procedure. I do this activity with every group irrespective of age but adapt it to the circumstances, whether the group is only meeting once or continually. A shortened version for a group only meeting once will involve distribution from a box of slips of paper. They will all have on them 'Have a good day' or similar, but one will say 'This is Your Day'. Selection is always a pleasant surprise. Adapt the procedure described for children. Even if people have not known each other for more than an hour it is always possible to find compliments. When it's your turn to have the cheers, whistling and clapping, do remain in eye contact and remember to keep breathing. From my observations of this scene happening lots of times I guess not many people get warmly acknowledged and appreciated very often and when it happens here, even so briefly, it can have a deep emotional effect. Tears have been known. And whatever you do make sure you take part in The Car Wash!

A list of necessary ground rules which need to be set for adult groups and the ways to introduce them are in the organisation section of Chapter 7.

5

Magic Circles

The Motivation for Circle Times and the original 1989 *TES* article

The 1989 *TES* article

> While parents possess the original key to their children's experiences, the spare key is held by the teachers.
>
> Haim Ginott, *Teacher and Child*

Children need to feel secure, know that they are appreciated as individuals and have a real sense of belonging to a group. These are the first three basic requirements for building self-esteem. Too many children walk into school each day with a less-than-acceptable level of self-esteem, as is evident from their attitudes, behaviour and preoccupations. Circle Times are often called Magic Circles because of the transformational effects on their participants. I believe the term 'Circle Time' was first used by others when bringing small groups of children together in a circle for social skills training. If resources allow, I can see the advantages of working with a small number at certain times, as in Circle of Friends when there are very particular difficulties to be tackled, but normally I think it is so much better to have the whole class together. It is the trust and security established in the whole class that helps every individual and gets the group dynamic to operate well.

Affective education, through Circle Time, helps children think more positively about themselves, gives them greater opportunities to be more responsible for themselves, and encourages and gives them skills to make better and wiser decisions. The intention is to go beyond helping children to feel good about themselves, important as that is. I certainly agree with William Purkey when he says that 'students who feel good about themselves and their abilities are the ones most likely to succeed' but, as I have already described, self-esteem is much wider than that.

> Even the most insensitive teacher will usually recognise and take into account a crippling physical handicap. Negative self-esteem, however, is often overlooked because we fail to take the time and effort it requires to be sensitive to how children see themselves and their abilities.
>
> W. Purkey, *Self-Concept and School Achievement*

Self-esteem, motivation, application and the ability to express yourself well are all essential for learning.

Julia Margo, Institute for Public Policy
Research, October 2007

Like all teachers, when I was a head teacher my aim was to help the children to learn readily and behave well. From my observation it became apparent that many were finding these two objectives increasingly difficult. I could see that many problems seemed to persist regardless of the efforts of highly competent, enthusiastic staff. It was obvious that some of the children often appeared less able than they really were and that much of the anti-social behaviour, both passive and aggressive, originated in an underlying lack of self-confidence. This was having a domino effect so that increasing numbers of children were being influenced in a negative way and staff energies and skills were being tested to the limit. If we had kept a register devoted to self-esteem many children would have been recorded believing themselves to be unloved, unwanted and rejected, feeling discouraged, powerless, inadequate and incompetent. This was clear from the things they said and did. They made comments such as:

'I hate it', 'There is never anything to do', 'This is stupid', 'No one plays with me', 'It's his fault'.

They could be seen showing off inappropriately, bullying and bragging, and constantly blaming others or they were obviously reluctant to express opinions, unwilling to take responsibility, or unwilling to try anything new. They were sometimes rude and lacked compassion; others were fearful and timid. These behaviours were clearly the product of low self-esteem and would keep them trapped in a downward spiral of failure and despair.

So the decision was taken to take more account of affective education in the school curriculum. What was set in motion was the grand plan of replacing the negative convictions with experiences which made them feel confident to deal with any problem they encountered and, as Branden says, feel totally worthy of happiness, success and respect. For a short time each day the academic schedule would be set aside. For many it would be the first time the children would realise the vital role that emotions play in their lives. This is where they would have the opportunity to try out new ones without fear of ridicule or criticism. They would come to enjoy the freedom of expressing an opinion on matters which concern their daily living and felt comfortable about listening to and respecting the views of others. The holistic way in Circle Times would show children gently but firmly, sensitively but clearly, how to use the skills which will enable them to see the difference between negative and productive positive behaviour. When this happens, where they previously acted in an aggressive or passive way, they can begin to see the advantages of assertiveness. Bullying will shrivel and wither away as the bullies gradually understand the reasons for that behaviour and with much support from the group get their needs met in non-harmful ways. Likewise, victims will get support and learn how to overcome difficult situations. Everyone will come to see the great value in friendship and relationships in the class will blossom. Peer pressure will become group support. Where harmony reigns, learning flourishes.

Because of the successes they gain in the classroom they will carry their self-confidence into adulthood and continue to use the skills they learnt in order to achieve it. It is not difficult to imagine how an appreciation of self and others generated in the classroom could begin to have a dramatic long-term effect on the future of society.

As I write, the government is arranging for the National Institute for Health and Clinical Excellence to develop well-being assessments for children. All children aged between four and 11 will be given questionnaires, jointly devised by the Universities of Warwick and Edinburgh, in which they will be asked if they feel optimistic, confident, loved and interested in others. They aim to monitor positive attributes such as confidence, resilience, attentiveness and the ability to form good relationships. This presents an opportunity to make a comparison of the answers from those pupils who have had the Circle Time experience and those that have not. There are difficulties in doing this, mainly dependent on the worth of the circles, the facilitation skills, the number of sessions involved, but it may still be worthwhile. Some years ago I attempted to do this on a very small scale and had university staff ready to help with the statistics, but unfortunately was unable to obtain funding. But, as you see, anecdotal evidence exists in abundance and is surely impossible to dismiss.

> This school isn't a good school because it's Catholic or it's selective. It's a good school because we know every child and we love them and care for them and we challenge them.
>
> Roisin Macguire, head teacher, St Joseph's College, Stoke–on–Trent, 'an outstanding leader' Ofsted (*Sunday Times*, November 2007)

When my article 'Magic Circles' was published in the *TES* in 1989 there was a massive positive response from readers from abroad as well as the UK, and an acknowledgement of the value of the participation of pupils in Circle Times was well established. The tremendous potential they had for good in the lives of children was clearly recognised by many teachers who adopted the idea and began to conduct their own circles. To avoid confusion, if I was writing it today I would make it clearer at the start that 'feel good' involves a sense of both worth and competence and I would need to expand on my remarks about the link between self-esteem and academic success.

Magic Circles

The following article appeared in the *Times Educational Supplement* on 30 June 1989 and is reprinted here with permission.

> In contemporary society low self-esteem should be considered an enormous public health problem. Patients who report low self-esteem usually say it has been present since early childhood, or at latest, adolescence. The rescue of a substantial proportion of the population from the misery of lifelong low esteem remains a challenge for both educationalists and mental health workers (*The Lancet*, 22 October 1988).

Research shows a strong correlation between a child's self-esteem and his or her academic success; statistics prove that children who feel good about themselves learn more easily and retain information longer. They do better in every way. If they have a sense of well-being they are much more likely to be able to handle the ups and downs of daily life, including prejudice, abuse, addiction, delinquency and violence.

With this belief in mind I instituted Circle Time in September 1988. For several years previous to this I had been taking classes and groups, spending time discussing behaviour, exploring feelings, playing games, with very pleasing results. Staff had commented on the changes the activities had brought about in the children, both individually and collectively, e.g. 'My class doesn't like playing yours' [addressed to the class teacher] 'at rounders. They always win. Your class seem to be able to work together so much better'.

I suggested to all the teachers that Circle Time begin each day, each class sitting on the floor in a circle. In some rooms there is space to do this without moving tables, in others this is done before the bell rings. If possible the teacher will be sitting first, waiting for the circle to form and able to greet each child individually on arrival. Before the register, the day begins with a round. The teacher says an incomplete sentence, gives an example to finish it off, then the child next to her repeats the phrase and puts his own ending to it, and so on. It has several purposes.

It is a re-establishment of the group, an important joining together into a class where membership is clearly acknowledged. Children can elect to 'pass' if they wish but few do – opportunity is given for them to come back at the end. Even in a large class the level of listening to others is clearly high. Some enjoy the chance to be really imaginative and direct in their answers. Many quickly recognise it as a safe environment where they can really say what they are thinking; e.g. 'Today I'm feeling … nervous' (a seven-year-old, two weeks into term). 'I wish I was with … my father, if I knew where he is' (a very shy 11-year-old girl). Sensitive teachers will hear these and respond appropriately in later interactions with the children. Even when a child tells the class that he is tired, that is an open acknowledgement of a fact and account can be taken of it.

Rounds are about all sorts of things, e.g. 'What makes me laugh is …'; 'My favourite TV programme is …'. Even a round where a child chooses a fruit she would like to be often reveals much. For the children, self-disclosure in these rounds by the teacher is very valuable too. Rounds help the retiring child to feel included. At the beginning of the term lots of activities are centred on getting to know each other (we are partially vertically grouped 7–9, 9–11 years) and on the creation of a close, warm class identity. 'I like it, Circle Time, you get to know all the children in the class really well' (a 10-year-old girl).

After registration and the opportunity to share with everyone anything that has happened during the time children have been apart, comes the selection of the 'special child' for the day. This is universally popular with the children and I would guess for many of them an unusual experience. The mother of an 11-year-old boy mentioned to her employer, who told me, that the previous day her son had told her that it had been his special day. 'I don't know what happened but it certainly did him good!' She had never made any other comment about her son's education in the whole of the previous three years. Another child, a very anxious eight-year-old girl, was seen to cry with happiness when she knew it was her turn to have a special day.

Selection is first made by balloon popping. Balloons are blown up, each child puts her name on a piece of paper inside a balloon, and the balloons are hung from the ceiling. Each day one balloon is popped and the child whose name appears is special child for the day. After every child had had a turn in this way another method – Riddles – was used, so that each had two special days in the term. Its importance in the children's lives was evident. On the second time round, one nine-year-old boy said 'It's Wednesday today and it was a Wednesday last time I was chosen'. Others chimed in, remembering the days of the week when it was their turn, and similar comments.

There is considerable opportunity for varying the procedure in dealing with the child of the day but the principles are clear. First, the child is presented (often by yesterday's holder) with a badge. In our case it is very simple, made of cardboard on string, but on one side it says 'I am Special' and on the other side 'I'm great', or something similar. Then she will be asked to leave the room while a discussion takes place inside about all the nice things which can be said about her (it is a real delight to me to see smiling children outside doors waiting to be called back) or alternatively she would immediately begin to ask children who volunteered by raising hands to make their comments. There are always plenty of contributions and the vast majority very genuine. The children receive them with quiet pleasure. Some make real discoveries. One 11-year-old boy was told by others that they admired his ability to calmly deal with problems (viz. aggressive situations). The next day the group was discussing 'feeling' words and he used 'surprised'. When asked to elaborate he said he had been surprised to find out how much he was liked. He has appeared to gain a lot of confidence and now joins in discussions much more freely than before.

Faced with a barrage of compliments it can be difficult to remember them or even believe them. It is important to get the children to preface their remarks with phrases like 'I think you ...', 'I believe that you ...', etc. In this way the recipient accepts it as an opinion and cannot contradict it. Teachers record the comments while they are being said and the sheet is presented to the child so that she can read them through later. Also, the child is asked to tell the class which comments mean most to them. 'You are nice to be with' is always a favourite. This part of the ceremony ends with the child asked to name and tell us one thing about herself of which she is pleased, perhaps proud. It often causes difficulty and here we see the measure of low self-esteem. I shall always remember the capable 11-year-old girl who eventually said in a low voice 'I am good at maths' and then in a whisper added 'sometimes'.

Part of the fun of Circle Time is that the special child is asked if he or she wants to be called by another name for the day. Nicknames used among friends become universally accepted and other children take bigger risks and choose their popular heroes and heroines. Special children are also given, or can claim, other privileges. One very popular one is to elect to sit on a chair at the front of assembly (held at 10.30); this means the whole school will acknowledge they are special. It has also become the custom for the special child to choose the game for the day. A repertoire of games has been built up and incorporated in Circle Time. These again have many purposes. One is to act as 'energy raisers'. They are useful at other times during the day as well. As an investment for the energy and enthusiasm given to the work which follows they are well worth the few minutes spent on them.

There are only three rules in Circle Time: only one person speaks at a time; everyone can have fun; no one can spoil anyone else's fun. It is a time when the children find out a bit more about themselves and what they are capable of and how they relate to each other. There are lots of serious, lively discussions where feelings are discovered, explored and accepted. The children come to realise that if they understand themselves it will help them to better understand others. The value of co-operation and friendship is examined and emphasised using practical exercises. At least twice a week in Circle Time each class splits into groups of three. This is the children's opportunity to talk and be listened to, where they will get close attention from peers to form and exchange ideas and opinions which are then brought back to the big group for an airing.

In school, of course, arguments, quarrels and unpleasant situations still abound as children follow their old patterns of behaviour in getting their needs met, but there is a growing awareness that there are alternatives. I believe children flourish when in an environment structured by definite controlled limits, but within these they must be encouraged to become responsible for their own decisions and helped to achieve autonomy. Self-esteem develops when children have a basis for evaluating present performance and making comparisons with earlier behaviour and attitudes.

Various sanctions and punishments are used. There is not space here to write about the importance of applying these appropriately so that they do not harm the child's self-concept. It is essential to differentiate between the doer and the deed, 'I like you but cannot accept your behaviour.'

Recently, two 11-year-old boys, not generally known for their community spirit or for their need to tell me anything, told me quite casually in the classroom while they were working how they had approached two younger boys in the playground who they knew were frightened of them and said 'OK, we'll be your friends'. They also volunteered the information that another boy (who sat there listening, a boy with a reputation for aggression) had gone out of his way to make friends with a first-year child and he confirmed it in a very unassuming manner.

Towards the end of term the emphasis was switched to goal-setting and achieving targets. Children were asked to think of small specific targets – things which they thought desirable for them to do or to learn to do, either at home or school, and to keep a daily record. With encouragement from everyone and the use of simple will exercises, the children were helped to realise how they could achieve their potential.

Visitors to Circle Time have been numerous and, sitting on the floor in the circle, are readily accepted by the children. Also the children were happy for a video to be made of parts of it, sponsored by the Artemis Trust. Other activities included taking photographs of every child and displaying them in the entrance hall for all to admire and the making of booklets called 'All About Me'. They have all been aimed at enhancing self-esteem.

The importance of self-esteem is stated very eloquently by Dorothy Corkille Briggs (1975):

A person's judgement of self influences the kinds of friends he chooses, how he gets along with others, the kind of person he marries, and how productive he will be. It affects his creativity, integrity, stability, and even whether he will be a leader or a follower. His feeling of self-worth forms the core of his personality and determines the use he makes of his aptitudes and abilities. His attitude toward himself is a direct bearing on how he lives all parts of his life. In fact, self-esteem is the mainspring that slates each of us for success or failure as a human being.

Starting the day with Circle Time

Special Day

For

Today's is

The reasons people like me are:

Certificate

for _____

This is what your class

think of you on your

Special Day

Activities in the Circles

The Special Day, discussions, brainstorming, rounds – banners, badges and books

We cannot assume that children have the skills they need in order to manage their emotions and meet our expectations about their behaviour. We need to take active steps to develop their social, emotional and behavioural skills. Whole school approaches linking behaviour and learning will become an increasingly common theme of government policy. The development of children's social, emotional and behavioural skills will focus on self-awareness, managing feelings, empathy, motivation and social skills.

Jean Gross, Director, National Primary Strategy,
DfES, October 2004

The Special Day

Special Days should be done at every Circle Time, first, because the effect in raising self-esteem is so apparent and, second, because it is a winner with the children!

The Special Day procedure is based on a formula aiming to promote a combination of a sense of security, identity and belonging at the same time. Its beginning always generates a lot of excitement. This is because the children know that one of them is to be selected to have a Special Day – this is just one reason why it's good to begin the day with Circle Time, although some teachers do it successfully at other times for organisational reasons. The child must be selected in a random way so there is an element of surprise. It must be seen to be fair. Everyone knows he or she will get a turn eventually; 'Special Days are all right because everyone gets a turn. I haven't been chosen yet but I'm looking forward to the day'.

There are many reasons why Circle Time should happen every day, although I well appreciate the pressures on the timetable. Apart from the opportunities for more personal growth each time it's done, if it starts each day the more likelihood that the children will discharge any stress that has been brought to school at that time, that they will re-connect to the security of the circle and their friends, and there will be less disruption and more work done during the rest of the day. The overriding reason for the children, however, is, I suspect, because it will bring their turn to have a Special Day that much closer. If Circle Time occurs every day, then it means that every child in an average-size class will have two Special Days a term, six a year. This is because the procedure is repeated once everyone has had a turn, using a different means of selection. If ever there was an activity which is universally popular and which benefits everyone then this is it.

One key way to get children to think positively about themselves is to get them to make positive statements to others. It has been shown quite clearly that one of the most effective ways of enhancing children's self-esteem is to get them to praise others. In his study, Brady showed improved scores for all children who took part. This Special Day procedure is an excellent vehicle for this to take place. When the child is selected, he or she is invited to sit in the middle of the circle. After the presentation of a badge which can then be worn all day so that it is a reminder to the rest of the class and can be used for identification purposes with the rest of the school, then the compliments can begin. All the children are invited to take turns to say things to this child which they think he or she would like to hear. All remarks should be prefaced by words such as 'I like ...', which will then indicate that it is the speaker's opinion, so that, for example, if the child is told that the speaker thinks he is clever or good-looking and that conflicts with a low estimate of himself, it cannot be subconsciously rejected. That is most important, otherwise a child with low self-esteem is unable to accept these statements. Obviously sincerity is the keynote; no one is forced to say anything they do not mean. A sensitive teacher can soon encourage the compliments to flow and even if the youngest children say they like the colour of the child's socks, it is a beginning and things soon progress. I think that the ordinary civilities are missing in so many children's lives today that even 'Good Morning. It's good to see you' is valuable. Lists of positive qualities displayed on a chart nearby can act as a reminder of compliments to consider. Things can always be found to be said to even the most unpopular child; children begin to look for the positive qualities which everyone has. For many, it's a new experience; society is awash with negativity and lots of children are immersed in it. In their homes, children often hear many more negative statements than positive ones.

Children who speak civilly to each other in the classroom are less likely to be aggressive to each other in the playground and elsewhere. Its effects on the reduction of bullying are substantial, as are other strategies employed in Circle Time. Good self-esteem will certainly lessen a child's need to bully. People who get negative attention don't think they can get positive attention or compliments. Bullies and trouble makers are making signals that they need some positive attention and when they get it in Circle Time – and it's here where you see how influential peers are – then the results can be dramatic. One session like this can be worth ten one-to-one sessions with an adult.

Equally important is that the potential victim is strengthened in Circle Time. Children move from each end of the passive–aggressive continuum and learn how to assert themselves in win–win situations. The benefits even extend to onlookers as they will certainly be inclined to intervene in a positive way in a bullying situation. High self-esteem encourages social responsibility; another result is less graffiti and vandalism.

Sometimes the repercussions go beyond the classroom. One teacher notes: 'Parents are coming to find out what is happening in the class to make the children so keen to get there'. Another says, 'Parents are asking for confirmation that the other children really did say all these things about their child and subsequently framing their Special Day certificates'. It is always interesting to ask the children which comments mean most to them.

This is a wonderful way to help a child gain a sense of security, identity and belonging: I have not met, or heard of, a child who has refused the opportunity to have a Special Day. Children all look forward to them immensely and seem to remember them vividly.

I have never known a child to complain about having to wait for a turn, or that the turn was over. All children know they will get a turn, although they have the excitement of not knowing when, and once it is over they know that their turn will come again. If we can help children to think positively about themselves, and to learn how they can take charge of their own lives, they will come to realise they can have a Special Day every day. We can help pupils to understand their own uniqueness:

What have a snowflake and a fingerprint in common?

Every one is unique.

What else is unique and special?

Every child; each one of us.

Procedure

The group should be sitting in a circle and a child randomly selected. The easiest method is to pick a name out of a hat, but there are much more imaginative ones.

One method is to give out balloons the day before Circle Time begins, one to each child. Before they are blown up and suspended from the ceiling, the child writes his name on a small piece of paper and drops it inside. The following day when everyone is ready, the pin is flourished, the balloon is popped and out drops the name of the child to have a Special Day.

When the balloons are finished the children can choose their own means of selection. Advent type calendars, with names behind the windows, are popular, so are panels of faces with names under the tongues. Names pushed into straws can be used, as can examples of children's writing put into unmarked envelopes which are pinned to the wall. A longer way is for children to draw a self-portrait on one side of paper, and riddles about themselves on the other. One can be selected daily, the portrait shown and the riddles read out while the group guesses who it is. The selection is usually made by the child who had the Special Day on the previous day.

The Special Day child is invited into the centre of the circle and presented with a badge or token of some kind on behalf of the group. These badges can be home-made or there are some appropriate commercial ones. Some children prefer to make their own. Children like wearing them. Suggested words for badges: 'Today is special!' and 'I am great!'

Either now or later, get the group to give the child a standing ovation – 30 seconds of clapping, cheering and whistles, offered with energy and enthusiasm! How many of us have this experience even once in a lifetime, and yet we all deserve it!

The Special Day child then sits in the middle of the circle and receives positive comments from the others in the group. Remember that these remarks and comments should be prefaced with 'I think ...' or 'I believe ...' etc., which stops the hearing child denying them at either a conscious or subconscious level. A great sense of belonging is given, and the Special Day child feels much appreciated, for example, 'He said he liked my smile', 'She said I was a nice person to be with'.

Until the class gets used to the idea it can be wise to invite the Special Day child to wait outside the door while a rehearsal takes place. This gives the adult a chance to hear the remarks beforehand and to prompt when necessary. It's the only time I know when children are gladly sent to stand outside the door! Comments should be recorded and presented for the child to keep. Name posters are one way of recording the Special Day comments; they look attractive displayed round the room.

Many of these may come to occupy a proud place in the bedroom at home.

Another approach is to have a list of qualities on display, for example, punctual, quick-thinking, persevering, and ask the children to tell the Special Day child which of those qualities apply to that child. The list acts as a reminder of some words to use. It can be added to all the time.

A very illuminating round is one where the stem is:

'The first thought I had when I knew it was going to be my Special Day was ...'

Examples of compliments given on Special Days and written on certificates:

Jumps high

Always helpful

My friend

Easy to be with

Skilled at soccer

Able to work well

Never loses her temper

Nice to go home with

Eager to help me

Keeps friends

Empathic

Likeable

Looks after her pets

You trust her

The Special Day child should then be invited to disclose something about themselves, for example, something he likes doing, making, collecting, reading, watching or eating. This will give a further feeling of affiliation to the group. Even though it is difficult for most, the child should also be encouraged to disclose something he has done or made of which he is pleased and proud: it is not bragging or boasting, it is not making comparisons with others; it does enhance self-esteem. We do a great disservice to our children if we do not teach them the difference between boasting and bragging and being proud of their achievements. One registers low, the other high self-esteem and they need to be able to recognise this.

The child can claim special privileges for the day. The badge is the passport to being able to do anything reasonable. They vary from school to school. If equipment is short then this is the child who has first turn, if he wants to sit on a chair at the front at assembly then he can do so, if he wants tea or coffee from the staffroom at break he may have it, if he wants to depart from the normal timetabled activity, perhaps with a friend, he may do so provided the work is done at some other time. The Special Day child can request 'A clap please'. This can be said in class at any reasonable time during the day, and a quick round of applause will follow. I have never known it to be abused, and it certainly brings lots of smiles. Another thing that the child can do is to choose the game which is normally played at this point. It is selected from a list of games which will promote self-esteem in some way. It doesn't take long, is an energiser for the beginning of the day and is great fun.

All children love to claim the privileges which are available on Special Days. Sitting in a specifically arranged row of chairs (remember there is one child from each class) at assembly is something they invariably enjoy. Their favourite lesson can be included in the day's timetable. No reasonable request will be refused. Some children offer to be friendly or help children they do not normally associate with. It encourages initiative and gives confidence to ask for what is wanted.

Discussion sessions are the times when children share with each other their thoughts, feelings, aspirations, etc. As part of the session a discussion could take place which considers possible new ways that the Special Day child may like to behave this day. A risk, taken with wisdom and skill, is a sure-fire way to enhance self-esteem. This Special Day routine, with its provision of an aware, caring environment, can be just what a child with a long record of failure and frustration needs to make a new beginning. An introverted child could be encouraged to be more assertive, knowing that the group is aware of his efforts and will be supportive. If a child can try out a new way of behaviour and break an old pattern which is holding back his true potential, this can lead to a realisation of being in control of his life.

Special Days are good for teachers too. They can be carried out in the classroom (you will find that children will want to arrange them as a surprise and will rig the selection procedure to achieve it) and in the staffroom. It's a really good experience when staff can say how much they appreciate each other. The privileges that can be claimed carry endless possibilities!

Schools may be the starkest example in modern society of an entire institution modeled after the assembly line. This has dramatically increased educational ability in our time, but it has also created many of the most intractable problems with which students, teachers and parents struggle to this day. If we want to change schools, it is unlikely to happen until we understand more deeply the core assumptions on which the industrial-age school is based.

Peter Senge, *Schools That Learn*

Discussions

Circle Time is an excellent forum for discussion. Discussions can benefit children in many ways. For example, children often have the mistaken belief that they alone experience the stresses of abuse, domestic violence, divorce, sibling rivalry, fear of failure, teasing, bullying, thinking themselves unattractive and so on. Discovering that they share the same longings, difficulties, conflicts and doubts enhances their self-esteem. Children will learn how to share and be comfortable with their feelings and this, in turn, may enable them to resist the problems of depression, drugs and alcohol. Instead of having sex education lessons in isolation, placing the subject into a talk and discussion in the middle of a Circle Time can result in positive benefits.

Discussions are most successful in small groups, later the class group is used for feedback and summing up. That way everyone will make an input even if they do not actually speak to the whole group. The way the small groups are formed is important. Allowing children to form their own is not a good idea except on certain occasions. Friends will always gravitate together and those without will suffer real anxiety. There will not be a healthy mix. Random groupings should be used. This can be done in many ways, for example, by asking the children to find others born in the same month, or who have the same initials or who are wearing different/the same colours. Three is the best psychological number for a group of this nature – a triad. Sometimes it is more appropriate to bring two triads together for feedback rather than immediately re-forming the big group. The use of these triads can be extended to activities other than those done in Circle Time, known as the Buddy System, it is a very powerful dynamic for encouraging a flourishing class atmosphere.

At the summing up stage with the whole group, it is good to record the conclusions in whatever way is most suitable. Posters put on display can be useful reminders where this is appropriate.

Circle Time is a good place for developing listening skills. Such skills are valuable in all relationships and, by and large, children do not get enough positive attention. Circle Time is a good opportunity for the shy and more isolated child to express himself, and be heard. When the child feels safe and concludes that judgements are not being made you will soon see he will be happy to join in and offer his two penny's worth. As respect and acceptance of each other grows in these discussions the skill of seeing the other's perspective increases and true empathy is present.

It is often not the most lovable individual who stands most in need of love, but the least lovable. Willed love often leads to liking.

Brainstorming

Q. How is dew formed?

A. The sun shines down and makes the leaves perspire.

Genuine response in GCSE exam 2006

Brainstorming is a valuable method to introduce to the class or group. A brainstorming session aims to generate ideas from a main theme and no matter how far-fetched, or trivial the ideas, the session will undoubtedly generate a lot of energy and good-natured argument. Discussion during Circle Time allows children to discover mutual likes and dislikes in sport, hobbies, music and the arts. Fighting, teasing, racial and gender incidents all get a good airing, and things said in Circle Time discussions can go a long way towards reducing the conflict and unpleasant behaviours found in most schools. For example, here is a list made by a class of nine-to-eleven-year-olds after a discussion which arose spontaneously from a remark made by one of the children:

Acceptable and non-acceptable punishments received at home

Non-acceptable

Slapped around face and head

Beaten with the dog's stick

Mouthful of cod liver oil to swallow

Mouthful of washing-up liquid (not to swallow)

Mouthful of washing-up liquid (forced to swallow)

Wash out mouth with soap

Locked in room with no food or drink

Acceptable

Slapped anywhere but face or head

Locked in room between meals

No television

No computer

Not allowed to play

No puddings

No sweets

No pocket money

Ignored

Rounds

A round is an excellent way of starting Circle Time. It is a highly visible way of bringing the children together at the beginning of the day, acknowledging each one's membership of the group and reminding them of the value of their relationship to others. When a group is new it is often useful to begin with a round which includes each person's name, for example, 'My name is ... and today I ...'. This is a good way of making a new member feel welcome, and visitors can be included easily into the group. Sentence stems which are left open for each child to complete, are a very powerful tool for helping the teachers to appreciate children's needs. Many statements that are made will lead to a better understanding of the child. It is important not to question or comment on statements during the round. If need be, issues can be dealt with at the end, or left for future class or small group discussions, or be discussed with the child privately.

The facilitator should always start. A sentence stem could be, 'Today I intend to be friendly by ...' [pause, now complete the stem], 'giving everyone I meet a smile'. Then repeat the stem, look at the child on the left or right, and they continue the round. Some children will say 'Pass' mainly because they need more time to think. They can be returned to at the end. Others need gentle encouragement. The number of passes diminishes as the group is established. Children that feel safe love this opportunity to speak to the class and it is usually high-quality listening time.

Rounds can often be used as an introduction or linked to the other activities that will take place in the Circle Time, for example, a sentence stem about animals can lead on to interesting movement and body work, a stem about 'What I'd like to be' can spark lively discussions on ambitions, careers, and the family system.

Some rounds to explore and encourage the sense of self-esteem

When I woke this morning my first thought was ...

As I walked to school today I was thinking of ...

When someone says something nice/nasty to me I feel ...

My favourite place at home is ...

My favourite place to play is ...

I feel really good/bad when ...

If I were a giant I would ...

If I were an animal/fruit/toy I would be a ...

If I could do anything I wanted I would ...

I hope that ...

I like it/don't like it when ...

I like/don't like people who …

If I could only have one thing (as much as I wanted) to eat/drink for the rest of the week I would choose …

Today I hope I shall be able to …

Today I would like to help a person/people to …

Today I would like someone to help me to …

I was very happy/sad/angry/scared when once …

I shall always remember the first time I …

If I could be invisible I would …

I would like the magic ring that …

School would be better if …

One of the best things about me is …

I like going to …

If I were the/a teacher I would …

I laugh when …

The last sentence stem can lead on to a laughing competition – who has the most contagious laugh? Making space for sharing jokes is popular. Apart from the need to share fun and humour, the ability to tell a story properly in order to get an appropriate reaction is a skill that needs practising.

Banners

There are five banners or signs, one for each set of circles. When you see one in the follow-up, get the children to make it in large letters big enough to display for all to see. Take time to explain and discuss the meaning, making sure they understand how it applies to them.

Badges

There are five badge shapes. As each set of five circles ends, get the children to stencil one or make one of a similar shape. In the middle there is space for each child to put a simple relevant catchphrase of their own choosing. Brainstorming would be good here.

Security, e.g. 'It's good here'.

Identity, e.g. 'It's me'.

Belonging, e.g. 'I have friends'.

Purpose, e.g. 'I will do it'.

Competence, e.g. 'I can do it'.

They are to act as positive reminders of what it is all about, what we are doing together. I think it is better if children make their own rather than use commercial badges. Something good made yourself always has more value in self-esteem terms than something shop bought. A lot of very useful art and craft activities can arise from Circle Times.

Books

In the follow-ups you will find some book titles. I strongly recommend you find time to read them to your circles as besides being wonderful stories they convey real self-esteem messages. I am sure all ages will enjoy them. You will know of other books too, or, if you are a storyteller, that's even better.

7

Circle Times for All

The teacher's role – circles to promote the five key issues relating to the possession of a high, healthy level of self-esteem

The teacher's role, a reminder

I have come to a frightening conclusion

I am the decisive element in the classroom

It is my personal approach that creates the climate

It is my daily mood that makes the weather.

As a teacher I possess tremendous power to make a child's life miserable or joyous.

I can be a tool of torture or an instrument of inspiration

I can humiliate or humor, hurt or heal.

In all situations, it is my response that decides whether a crisis will be escalated or de-escalated, and the child humanized or de-humanized.

Haim Ginott, *Teacher and Child*

Circle Time is like the scaffolding which is erected to support a building while it is being built, it supports the children while they grow and develop their esteem. The teacher is the architect who plans and devises the activities and uses all her skill and experience to give information and assurance at the level the children need. If your intention is to allow the children to grow by experiencing the five stages necessary for self-esteem, then you will gently and firmly give them the power to take risks, consider options, make choices and decisions, all in the safe environment of Circle Time.

In an ideal world every teacher would have the opportunity to participate in an adult Circle Time. Here, he or she would see how helpful it would be for them to practise their facilitation skills, understand group dynamics, hone their observation and reflective listening talents, find out about body language, see emotional literacy in action and enhance their own charismatic presence. Above all they would discover real empowerment for themselves. One of the multitude of benefits of this gift is that teachers are then always able to appreciate the needs and reactions of their precious charges and truly transformatory Circle Times take place. Time spent on appropriate training is of immense value. The qualities discovered and embraced and the skills learnt will be found to be life enhancing, a boon both professionally and personally.

I would never advise that a teacher should be asked to undertake responsibility for Circle Times unless she felt absolutely comfortable in doing so. A key resource for success is the self-esteem of the facilitator. Doing the activities described in Chapter 2 will be found to be useful indicators and the checklist in Chapter 3 gives guidance on their application in facilitation. I would certainly support Circle Time being facilitated by Teaching Assistants where appropriate. I am sure many have the skills and qualities to do so. I would be unhappy, though, if Circle Time was then put into preparation time and the teacher was absent from the proceedings. This is key relationship time for both teacher and pupils. If you want, let the assistant facilitate and the teacher join in, not watching but taking part.

You have to be a special person to be a student-centred teacher

Teachers always need the ability to express themselves in a simple organised manner; never more so than in Circle Time. Lectures are avoided. The golden rule is short and concise verbal input, with active participation by everyone. Perhaps the most important of all is the ability to connect with the child in one's adult self. Roald Dahl, the author of so many wonderful books for the young, had the gift of experiencing life through the eyes and ears of a child and for that he will always be remembered.

Circle Time success comes from establishing excellent relationships between teacher and children. Those who imagine it has to have a 'mumsy', lovey-dovey, goody-goody approach are quite mistaken.

Here are some opinions from teachers who conduct Circle Times:

> *I think the majority of teachers believe that being positive, honest and fair with children is fundamental to good classroom practice. Circle Time and the Special Day procedure give teachers a vehicle, a means to carry out those beliefs in a structured and controlled way.*

> *It has increased my awareness of what matters to children and how they see things.*

> *It makes them feel important. I discovered all sorts of things about them.*

Circles to promote the five key issues relating to the possession of a high healthy level of self-esteem

Many of the original activities have been updated and new ones will be found in both the circles and the well-being section. The terms 'child' and 'children' have been retained from the circles in the first edition but you will find most activities are easy to use or to adapt with participants of any age. There are a few clearly more suitable for young circlers and others best used by older teens and adults. The first two circles are designed to take this into account and you can decide whichever you think most appropriate to use in order to get your series of circles off to a good start. There are also activities for older participants to be found in Chapter 2.

When using the visualisations do remember that for children or adults that have not experienced guided imagery before, the best introduction to it is available in the first three sections of the CD. Also bear in mind that the benefits happen when they are repeated a number of times.

Activities put in the follow-up sections are for use either within the Circle Times or on other occasions. The activities in the well-being section can be used in any Circle Time if required or separately at any time.

Organisation – things to consider before you start

Sitting
The floor or chairs? For Circle Times with children, I chose the floor every time. Circle Time is for the benefit of the children, remember, and that's where they like to be and of course adults must be there with them. The children can jiggle about and be comfortable without distracting you. Everyone is closer, which is very important. When the time comes to get up to have an activity there is no time lost moving the chairs. Stack them in the corner before you start. The older the participants I suppose you may have to give way to chairs but opt for the floor whenever you can. Try it and see the difference it makes. As the leader, take your shoes off, be on the floor first and greet each person by name or a smile as they sit and join the circle. It is always interesting to see who opts to sit next to the leader and who chooses to be on the far side of the circle. This will not stay static for long as after a movement activity people will usually wish to sit next to their new partners. Never have long periods of sitting still whether it is on the floor or chairs. Movement and action can do wonders for self-esteem.

Talking
Children can be told about the Melanesians who used a conch shell, in which, when held to the ear, the sound of the sea was heard. It was a symbol, reminding everyone that the person who held it in their hands spoke while everyone else listened. If you want to use an object for this reason a beanbag makes a useful substitute because if need be it can be thrown across the circle. To ring the changes sometimes someone can bring something especially from home to be used. I prefer not to have anything to pass around for this purpose. It can be used as a novelty for very young children but otherwise it is often just a distraction which slows up thoughts and holds up great contributions.

Rules for children

Wait until Circle Time for Security 2 on p. 79 and follow the suggestions. Within reason do let them own their Circle Time rules. Where children are involved in making rules and setting standards they are more likely to follow them. Every opportunity should be taken in schools to empower children to take responsibility for themselves. It should be understood that the rules must be based on truth, trust, responsibility, active listening and no put-downs. For those who find it difficult to keep set rules and standards, there are many strategies available which will not diminish self-esteem and yet have the desired effect. Sanctions should always be appropriate to the offence and be dealt with privately.

Rules negotiated by a group of 11-year-olds

1   Listen to what other people say.

2   Don't be nasty to each other.

3   No talking when someone else is talking.

4   Be kind to each other and give support.

5   If all you can say is something unpleasant, don't say anything.

6   If people don't want to say anything they don't have to.

7   Don't laugh at what other people say.

8   Think before you ask a question.

Rules for older pupils and adults

Use Circle Time for Security 1A, p. 76. If you are just having a one-off session, i.e. a day workshop, or starting on a series of circles, the procedure is important to follow if the sessions are to be successful.

Visitors

Circle Time is not a spectator sport. Visitors and guests must join in the circle and take a full part in all the activities. That way they will best be able to judge the value of the process and everyone else will not feel inhibited and will be able to participate fully.

Behaviour

Allow shy children their own time to join in without pressure. Passes in rounds are fine but always go back and give another opportunity as it may just have been time that was wanted. Anti-social behaviour can be dealt with in several ways. Look for the reasons. Address any anxieties first. Unless extreme, ignore, and praise others. Another is to address the child directly, e.g. 'Thank you for not talking' and look elsewhere immediately with the presumption it will be done. It usually is. Another is to ask the group to remind you of the rules, tell you if they believe they are necessary and then ask children to ask the culprit, in a warm inviting manner, to really join in and enjoy the session. It can be difficult to resist when you are wanted. There are lots of variations. Try hard not to exclude. Use smiles not frowns whenever you possibly can.

Starting

If you are about to begin on a series of Circle Times do use the following five sections in the order presented. Children and people need to feel secure before they can move on to other competencies. Experienced users will, as they become familiar with the resource, modify the activities to suit the needs of members of the group. When the routines are established and the theory understood, teachers can diagnose elements that are lacking in individual children, and strategies can be devised and built into Circle Time which will help particular pupils.

The circle shape is obviously crucial. It represents mutual respect and equal participation and involvement in decision-making.

> The significance of the circle: the circle as a symbol of self. It expresses the totality of the psyche in all its aspects, including the relationship between man and the whole of nature. Whether the symbol of the circle appears in primitive sun worship or modern religion, in myths or in dreams, in the mandala drawn by Tibetan monks ... it always points to the single most vital aspect of life ... its ultimate wholeness. Roundness (the mandala motif) generally symbolises a natural wholeness. The round table, incidentally, is a well-known symbol of wholeness and plays a role in mythology – King Arthur's round table.
>
> Aniela Jaffe, *Man and His Symbols*

The Circles

1 A variety of activities to enhance a sense of security.

2 A mixture of activities to foster a sense a sense of identity.

3 An assortment of activities to cultivate a sense of belonging.

4 A collection of activities to inspire a sense of purpose.

5 A selection of activities to maintain and enjoy a sense of competence.

6 An album of activities to nourish a sense of well-being.

Each section has a number of separate Circle Time sessions except for the sixth section.

Key to icons

These icons help to identify each activity with its source section. For repeated activities such as the Lighthouse and Plan for the day, a full description will be given in the first circle and an icon will be used thereafter.

 Selection of child and the making of the Special Day

 Round – a good way to start Circle Time

 Discussions – thinking, participation, debates, involvement, making decisions

 Game – raising energy/fun level

 Activity – a little self-esteem

 Group yell – a real energiser

Circle squeeze – quiet, warm beginnings

 Physical contact in a variety of ways

 Visualisation/guided imagery

 The Lighthouse – an essential ending, closure

 Plan for the day – moving on

Circle Time to promote a sense of security 1

For children

> Children don't care how much you know
>
> Until they know how much you care

Opening round

'Good morning, everyone. A special person in my life is ... .'

or

'Someone I really like to be with ... .'

(The completion can be either a name or a relationship.)

Selection of child

Hello name game

Use a cushion or beanbag to throw across the circle to someone, as you do so say the person's name preceded by a greeting, like, 'Hi', 'Hello', 'Good morning'. Encourage the children to think of their own greetings. These are simple but positive statements, and there should be good eye contact. Some children have nicknames which they like and are known only to a few friends. They can be invited to share these with the group. Be sure that everyone is included. Tell the children that if there is someone whose name they do not know, to ask for it, and then throw the cushion to that person.

This game is done most effectively standing. One version, which has the merit of speed, is to sit down when you've thrown the cushion. It can then be played against the clock, but the cushion has to be thrown across the circle and not passed to a neighbour.

New friends

Introduce the discussion by asking the whole group the following question: 'If you are meeting someone for the first time what do you think you should get to know about them?' Then prompt them, if necessary, with some of the following questions:

'What do teachers want to know about you when you start school? If you have ever moved into a new house, how do you get to know your neighbours? What is the first thing you say to them? If a new child comes into the class what do you think you would know about them by the end of the first day? By the end of the term? What would you like them to know about you?'

'Meeting a new person can be a real adventure. Just think of it. You may be talking to someone who is going to become your best friend for the rest of your life!'

Choosing a partner

'Look around the circle and decide on a few people who you do not know very well. I wonder if the ones you don't know have a per or not, or what they like to do on Saturdays. Get up and go and ask one of them to be your partner. Find a space where you can sit next to each other, but as far away from everyone else as possible.'

or

'I would like you to get up and see if you can find one of the people in the group who lives the furthest away from you. Ask that person to be your partner and then find a space where you can sit next to each other, but as far away from everyone else as possible.'

or

'I would like you to get up and find a partner who you have not spoken to since yesterday. With your partner find a space ...'

Distribute interview sheets (page 75) and pencils.

'Decide which of you will be A and which B. Hands up A. Hands up B. A will be the interviewer first and will ask B the questions on the sheet. Either write the answers down or remember in your head, whichever is easier. You don't have to ask the questions in that order' (if there are any children with reading difficulties, this is the time to read them aloud), 'and you can ask other questions if you wish. They do not have to answer any questions they don't wish to. Is that clear? Any questions?

'I am going to give you a few minutes' (your decisions will depend on maturity of children) 'then I shall ask if you have had enough time. In a little while it will be time to change over and for B to be the interviewer. When we have all finished I shall ask you to introduce your partner to the group.'

It is important not to rush this activity. Be ready to encourage some of the children. The slow starters often become the most involved.

When the interviewing has finished, the partners can introduce each other to the group. This activity can also be done in triads, two children sharing the questioning of the third. This method takes the pressure off reporting back to the group. This is a time-consuming activity, but very worthwhile, especially at the beginning of a school year or the formation of a new group.

At the end tell them that you have planned a lesson in which they can work together that day so that they can get to know even more about each other.

 ## Lighthouse

All hold hands and do a Lighthouse. Remind children that the light from a Lighthouse shines in order to help people. It shines in a friendly way helping everyone that is near it. Ask everyone to look around the circle, make eye contact with some, and smile. This should be a quick activity and done silently. It stops when the hands are parted, which the teacher initiates.

Plan for the day

At the end of each Circle Time (if it's done at the beginning of the day) before anyone gets up, take the opportunity to announce what the plan for the rest of the day will be, to involve the children in the organisation, to remind them of equipment needed and where to find it, to tell them where they need to be at particular times, for example, appointments for doctors or swimming lessons. Wish everyone a happy and productive day. Do the children have any questions or comments?

Ask your partner:

What is your full name?

Do you have a nickname?

What do you like to be called?

How old are you?

When is your birthday?

Who do you live with?

What are their names?

If you have brothers and sisters how old are they?

Where do you live?

How long have you lived there?

How do you get to school – walking, bicycle, bus, car?

What are your interests outside school?

Do you belong to any clubs, teams?

What games do you like?

What are your favourite television programmes?

Do you read any comics; if so which ones?

Do you borrow books from the local library?

Do you have pocket money; if so how much?

Do you have to do anything for your pocket money?

Did you go away on holiday this year?

If you could go anywhere in the world you wanted to next year, where would you go?

Who would you go with?

If you could be any age, what age would you like to be?

Do you wish you had a larger family or a smaller family, or is your family just the right size?

Do you ever get teased? Do you ever tease others?

Will you smoke when you grow up? Why?

If there is one thing you could change, what would it be?

Who is the best teacher you have ever had? Why?

Do you enjoy being at school? Is there anything you would like to change about school?

Is there one thing which you would like to learn how to do better?

There will be lots of other questions you can think of. Remember, they should only be ones which you wouldn't mind someone asking you.

The person being asked the questions can always says 'Pass' if he or she wants to.

Circle Time to promote a sense of security 1 A

For older teens and adults

> Experiential learning involves expanding your ability to produce the results you want in life.
>
> Peter Senge, *The Fifth Discipline*

Opening round

'My favourite place is ... .'

or

'I like it when ... .'

Round

Introducing partner to group.

If the participants are unknown to each other ask them to pair with their neighbour and take five minutes to exchange details about themselves so that they can then introduce each other to the group. If age appropriate they should say why they have come to the group, what they wish to gain from attendance and if they have attended similar groups.

Circle round introducing partners to group.

Ground rules

Partners join with another pair and discuss the following.

'The way I would like it to be in this group today so that I will

- feel at ease and enjoy other people's company and

- absorb and learn what is being dealt with is ... .'

In whole group members then offer rules which should include:

- Confidentiality. What is said in the group must remain in the group unless agreed otherwise.

- Members must remember to be non-judgemental at all times.

- Listen without interrupting when someone is speaking.

- Pass at any time. No need to share (but ask yourself why).

- Speak in the first person singular, not 'one', 'you' or 'we'.

- Address others directly in second person, not 'him' or 'her'.

- Take responsibility for own experience.

- Administration – breaks, drinks, toilets, handouts.

Display Johari Window (page 7). Point out that in order to learn more about yourself and others, disclose what is going on inside and be open to others doing the same.

Getting to know you

'Everyone please put your hands up in the air and then show your choice of any numbers of fingers and thumbs between one and ten. Leave out any friends and people that introduced you. Please find two others with the same number of fingers on display as yourself. Then go and sit down together.

'What you have to do now is find out all the things you have in common. They have to be unusual things, such as where you went for a holiday or having the same house number. You only have three minutes so you have to talk fast. There is one more rule. Each time you do find something in common you must all shout "Yes" in a loud voice before you go on to the next. When you have got to the tenth one please jump up, shout "Yes, Yes, Yes, We've done it!" and then sit again.

'Is that clear? Any questions? Go!'

When all the triads have completed they stay in position. Ask what it was like for them. Was it fun?

When we can be relaxed and playful we are more likely to be receptive and unafraid.

Sentence completion

In same triads each person takes a turn to complete 'I think self-esteem is …'. Go round six times with a different ending each time. Then triad discusses to see if they can arrive at a common definition. State how long they have to do this. At end say 'One more minute.'

'Now I would like you to take it in turns, just one round to complete "I think my self-esteem is …" Give as long or short an answer as you wish.' Again state time given to do this and warn as time is ending.

Bring everyone back to whole group and ask each triad to give their definition of self-esteem. Write up answers. Display self-esteem definitions given in Chapter 1 and point out common misunderstandings about the term. Allow general discussion.

Walking therapy

See Chapter 8, circles to promote a sense of well-being

My learning today

Share these thoughts with a partner or the whole group:

The three things I have learnt today are …

I shall implement them by doing …

I shall probably sabotage them by doing …

Lighthouse

All hold hands and do a Lighthouse. Remind children that the light from a Lighthouse shines in order to help people. It shines in a friendly way, helping everyone that is near it. Ask everyone to look around the circle, make eye contact with some, and smile. This should be a quick activity and done silently. It stops when the hands are parted, which the teacher initiates.

Plan for the day

At the end of each Circle Time (if it's done at the beginning of the day) before anyone gets up, take the opportunity to announce what the plan for the rest of the day will be, to involve the children in the organisation, to remind them of equipment needed and where to find it, to tell them where they need to be at particular times, for example, appointments for doctors or swimming lessons. Wish everyone a happy and productive day. Do the children have any questions or comments?

Follow-up

Have 'My learning today' at the end of every circle for adults and teens.

Circle Time to promote a sense of security 2

 ### Opening round

'I think the most important rule that we have in school is ... .'

 ### Selection of child

 ### Who moved?

A child goes outside the room and returns to guess who changed places in the interim. Lots of variations can make it easier or harder and therefore a safe risk for some and a bigger challenge for others.

 ### Rules

Generate the discussion by using the following ideas as prompts.

'What are rules, and why do we have them? Imagine a school with no rules. What would be the advantages and disadvantages? Do all schools have the same rules? Has anyone experience of another school?'

'Rules are best made by the people to whom they will apply. Are the laws in China or Japan the same as in this country? Can you imagine the government in those countries telling us about traffic laws?' Ask for examples.

'So, what are our school rules?' The teacher or a volunteer writes them on a list as they are offered and adds any not mentioned. 'School rules apply to everyone in this school, but we as a group need our own rules. We call them ground rules or basic rules and they must apply to everyone. By respecting the ground rules we have set ourselves we can feel safe and secure within our group. Every one of us is unique, as we know. I know what rules I would like, but they might not be the ones you want, so let's find out what each other's rules would be.

'I want you to work with two other people and make a list of the rules you would like. After a little while we'll come back together and make a combined list.'

A free choice of partners is recommended for this activity.

 At the end, receive all suggestions for rules without comment. Invite children to discuss them. Remind them of the advantages of having few rules. Can they recommend any rules that could be pruned from the list? Finally, ask if all the rules on the list can be agreed unanimously. Remind them of the British system of majority votes and the ways we make laws. Ask that everyone accepts the final list, a show of hands or similar gesture is helpful, and then say that these ground rules operate from this time on. For example, Circle Time rules:

1 Only one person speaks at a time.

2 Don't spoil anyone's fun.

3 Have fun yourself!

Lighthouse

All hold hands and do a Lighthouse. Remind children that the light from a Lighthouse shines in order to help people. It shines in a friendly way, helping everyone that is near it. Ask everyone to look around the circle, make eye contact with some, and smile. This should be a quick activity and done silently. It stops when the hands are parted, which the teacher initiates.

Plan for the day

At the end of each Circle Time (if it's done at the beginning of the day) before anyone gets up, take the opportunity to announce what the plan for the rest of the day will be, to involve the children in the organisation, to remind them of equipment needed and where to find it, to tell them where they need to be at particular times, for example, appointments for doctors or swimming lessons. Wish everyone a happy and productive day. Do the children have any questions or comments?

Follow-up

Banner: Everyone needs time to think and learn.

Display and fix in permanent position. Ask what this saying means. Why is it important for us all to remember?

Circle Time to promote a sense of security 3

Opening round

'My name is ... and today I wish ... .'

Selection of child

Who is this?

A child volunteers to sit in front of another in the circle but not before the latter has shut his eyes. He keeps them closed, stretches his arms out and uses his hands to feel the head and features of the other, trying to guess who it is. Make sure everyone gets a turn, but not necessarily on the same day. (Can be done two or three couples at a time.)

Secrets

'Today I'm going to give each of you a piece of paper and I would like you to go and sit where you can write on it without being overlooked.' The group disperses and a piece of paper is distributed to each child. 'This game is called secrets. I would like you to think of a secret which you are willing to share with this group. You write it on this paper, but you do not put your name on it. What sort of secrets should you write? You can say things which you really hate, or which you like very much, or what you are afraid of. People have all kinds of secrets. I will give you a minute to think. When you have written your secrets we jumble all the paper up in this box. Sitting in a circle I shall take out one at a time and read it to the group. Even if I recognise the writing I shall never reveal the author's name. What we do then is to guess who wrote it. It will remain up to you to decide if you tell us it is your secret; I hope you will feel able to.'

In this activity it is important for teachers to participate. Disclosing an anxiety will certainly help children to share their own. The secrets are read out and shared. At the end pose the question: 'How did you feel sharing your secret with us?' Give some time for discussion.

Lighthouse

All hold hands and do a Lighthouse. Remind children that the light from a Lighthouse shines in order to help people. It shines in a friendly way, helping everyone that is near it. Ask everyone to look around the circle, make eye contact with some, and smile. This should be a quick activity and done silently. It stops when the hands are parted, which the teacher initiates.

Plan for the day

At the end of each Circle Time (if it's done at the beginning of the day) before anyone gets up, take the opportunity to announce what the plan for the rest of the day will be, to involve the children in the organisation, to remind them of equipment needed and where to find it, to tell them where they need to be at particular times, for example, appointments for doctors or swimming lessons. Wish everyone a happy and productive day. Do the children have any questions or comments?

Follow-up

The Velveteen Rabbit by Margery Williams. Written in 1922 and in print in many different editions since. Every group, young and old, needs this read aloud.

'Once you become real you cannot become unreal again. It lasts for always.'

Question: What does it mean to be real?

Circle Time to promote a sense of security 4

Opening round

'Good morning everyone. If I were the king/queen/prime minister I would... .'

Selection of child

Name game

The child on the left begins by saying his name, for example 'My name is John'. The child on his left then says 'Your name is John, I am Kate'. The next one says 'You are John, you are Kate and I am Sarah', and so on. It's absolutely acceptable if someone cannot remember and has to ask to be reminded someone's name – except for you! Your turn is last, of course, and you can make a big fuss of each child as you say their name – you could get up and shake each one by the hand, or pretend to get mixed up, or prefix each name with 'the great', 'the wonderful', 'the super', 'the marvelelous', etc. This is a good opportunity to say that you appreciate them all.

Telling you about me

Produce a ball of string or wool. Hold the end and make a personal disclosure of some kind, for example 'The name of the book I am reading at the moment is ...', or 'I am looking forward to doing ... with ...', then pass the ball to someone else who does the same, and so on, creating a web around the circle.

As the ball is rewound the children can be asked if they can remember who said what.

The Quick Relax

It would be very appropriate to do this activity here.

See Chapter 9, page 146

Lighthouse

All hold hands and do a Lighthouse. Remind children that the light from a Lighthouse shines in order to help people. It shines in a friendly way, helping everyone that is near it. Ask everyone to look around the circle, make eye contact with some, and smile. This should be a quick activity and done silently. It stops when the hands are parted, which the teacher initiates.

Plan for the day

At the end of each Circle Time (if it's done at the beginning of the day) before anyone gets up, take the opportunity to announce what the plan for the rest of the day will be, to involve the children in the organisation, to remind them of equipment needed and where to find it, to tell them where they need to be at particular times, for example, appointments for doctors or swimming lessons. Wish everyone a happy and productive day. Do the children have any questions or comments?

Follow-up

My security badge.

Circle Time to promote a sense of identity 1

Emotionally intelligent children are better able to recognize their own emotional stress, better at sorting themselves when upset, better at focusing attention and better at understanding people.

John Gottman, *The Heart of Parenting*

Noisy or quiet ?

'How would everyone like to start today? You can choose to have a noisy one or a quiet one. I see some want a noisy one and others want a quiet one, so let's do both, the noisy one first.'

The big yell

'Everyone stand. Watch me. Bend your knees but stay on your toes and touch the floor with the tips of your fingers. Now we begin to hum as we slowly unwind, straighten up getting louder and louder and when we are up tall again jump as high as you can and yell, making a big, big noise. Now all together "That was good". Now we will do it three times non-stop, getting louder every time. Well done. Everyone sit please.'

Circle message

'Everyone join hands. Now I am going to give a secret number of squeezes to the hand of the person next to me. That person has to pass them on and so on round the circle till it comes back to me from the other person next to me. The test is to see if the message that returns is the same one that I sent.'

Let someone else have a turn at sending a message.

Round

'One of the best things that has ever happened to me is when … .'

Selection of child

Liar

Child A mimes an activity, for example, writing. B asks 'What are you doing?' A answers untruthfully, for example, 'Playing football'. B then has to mime playing football, and when asked what he is doing by C, B answers untruthfully, and so on round the circle.

Feelings

Produce photos, drawings or masks showing the same face but each looking very different.

'What is happening when you look at this face? It's the same one but it looks different each time. It is because something inside us changes.

'What are these changes called? So what do the faces show?

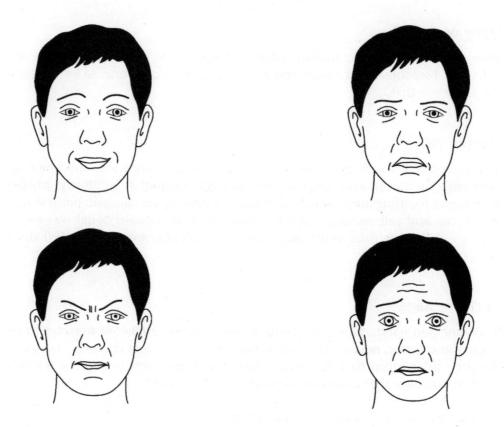

'Being happy, sad, angry and frightened.

'Can you think of other words with the same meaning as these?

'Have a look around, do you think anyone in this circle does not have feelings? Do you think I have feelings?'

It very much depends on the age and maturity of the children whether small groups are used at this point. If small groups are used, I would ask the children to find two others, perhaps with the same colour hair. Then they should take it in turns to tell the others:

'I can think of a time when I was happy. It was when … .'

If it's been decided not to divide the children into small groups, ask for volunteers to begin. If there have been small groups, then give the opportunity for those that want to, to share with the large group at the end.

The teacher or leader can ask the children if it's all right and natural, for example, to feel angry. It's important to help the children realise that all kinds of feelings are acceptable. They are a very important part of everyone. They are not good, bad, right or wrong.

'Do robots have feelings? When we see them on television or in films it sometimes looks as if they have. What about cartoon characters? Do they have feelings? But when they are drawn they certainly show feelings, don't they? If they did not they would be very uninteresting to watch.'

Stretching

'Who can demonstrate what a really good stretch looks like? Yes, all your fingers and toes then your arms and legs, jiggle them, move them, chest out, head slowly up and down. Now I would like everyone to stand, stretch as much as possible, have a long stretch, make yourself bigger everywhere, then crouch down. Wait there a minute. How do you feel as you crouch down? Then have one big jump, clap your hands above your head, and we will all sit down again in the circle.'

Lighthouse

All hold hands and do a Lighthouse. Remind children that the light from a Lighthouse shines in order to help people. It shines in a friendly way, helping everyone that is near it. Ask everyone to look around the circle, make eye contact with some, and smile. This should be a quick activity and done silently. It stops when the hands are parted, which the teacher initiates.

Plan for the day

At the end of each Circle Time (if it's done at the beginning of the day) before anyone gets up, take the opportunity to announce what the plan for the rest of the day will be, to involve the children in the organisation, to remind them of equipment needed and where to find it, to tell them where they need to be at particular times, for example, appointments for doctors or swimming lessons. Wish everyone a happy and productive day. Do the children have any questions or comments?

Follow-up

Banner: Everyone learns at their own speed in their own ways.

Circle Time to promote a sense of identity 2

The big yell

'Everyone stand. Watch me. Bend your knees but stay on your toes and touch the floor with the tips of your fingers. Now we begin to hum as we slowly unwind, straighten up getting louder and louder and when we are up tall again jump as high as you can and yell making a big, big noise. Now all together, "That was good". Now we will do it three times non-stop, getting louder every time. Well done. Everyone sit please.'

or

Circle message

Everyone join hands. Now I am going to give a secret number of squeezes to the hand of the person next to me. That person has to pass them on and so on round the circle till it comes back to me from the other person next to me. The test is to see if the message that returns is the same one that I sent.'

Let someone else have a turn at sending a message.

Round

'I' m ...' (name) 'and today I'm feeling ...'.

Selection of child

Sculpting in threes

A is the sculptor; B is the model; C is the clay. A closes her eyes; B adopts a pose and stays in that pose. A has to feel B and then turn to C and put her in the same position. When all the As have finished they open their eyes and everyone decides how accurate the sculptors have been. Take turns to be sculptors, models or clay.

School feelings

Group the children in pairs and give each pair a piece of blank paper. 'Draw four columns on your piece of paper and head each column: happy, sad, angry and scared. Under each heading make a list of what things in this school give you these feelings. Think of all the things which happen to you from the time you arrive in the morning until you leave, not just in the classroom, but in the hall, corridor, toilets and playground. Then bring your lists back to the group where we will share them and see if they are similar or different.'

This can lead to a large group discussion from which will undoubtedly emerge topics such as bullying and fairness. Let it be known that teachers' behaviour as well as that of other pupils can be discussed if it's appropriate. If necessary, these topics can be dealt with in further sessions.

Lighthouse

All hold hands and do a Lighthouse. Remind children that the light from a Lighthouse shines in order to help people. It shines in a friendly way, helping everyone that is near it. Ask everyone to look around the circle, make eye contact with some, and smile. This should be a quick activity and done silently. It stops when the hands are parted, which the teacher initiates.

Plan for the day

At the end of each Circle Time (if it's done at the beginning of the day) before anyone gets up, take the opportunity to announce what the plan for the rest of the day will be, to involve the children in the organisation, to remind them of equipment needed and where to find it, to tell them where they need to be at particular times, for example, appointments for doctors or swimming lessons. Wish everyone a happy and productive day. Do the children have any questions or comments?

Follow-up

The Shrinking of Treehorn, by Florence Parry Heide. The first of the Treehorn trilogy and in print for 33 years. It not only speaks about the insecurities of childhood but 'hits a chord with adults as well as when they read it they realise, that's true, I am not paying children enough attention'.

Circle Time to promote a sense of identity 3

The big yell

'Everyone stand Watch me. Bend your knees but stay on your toes and touch the floor with the tips of your fingers. Now we begin to hum as we slowly unwind, straighten up getting louder and louder and when we are up tall again jump as high as you can and yell, making a big, big noise. Now all together, "That was good". Now we will do it three times non-stop, getting louder every time. Well done. Everyone sit please.'

or

Circle message

Everyone join hands. Now I am going to give a secret number of squeezes to the hand of the person next to me. That person has to pass them on and so on round the circle till it comes back to me from the other person next to me. The test is to see if the message that returns is the same one that I sent.'

Let someone else have a turn at sending a message.

Round

'If I were a famous person I would be ...'.

Selection of child

Train name game

The children stand and imagine they are passengers waiting at different railway stations. The teacher in the middle of the circle is the train warming up. After a few preliminary circlings she goes to a station to pick up the first passenger. She says 'Good morning, what is your name?' The child answers, whereupon the teacher shouts the name five times, at the same time jumping and clapping hands. She then turns round and puts her hands on the child's waist and they shuffle off to pick up the next passenger. The first child says 'Good morning, what is your name?' The second child answers, whereupon the teacher and first child shout the second name five times and jump up and down. When the second child is collected, the train turns so the second child is in the front and has to ask for the next child's name. Everyone on the train shouts the name of the new passenger and jumps up and down. As the train gets longer it can be split into several trains to make the game quicker!

Feelings and actions

The teacher mimes an emotion, for example, anger, by shouting, growling, flinging arms about, or joy, by smiling, laughing, jumping. Exaggerate all your movements and walk round the circle. Ask for a volunteer (A) to come out and mimic you, and then ask if they can mime the opposite feeling. A then mimes a new emotion and chooses B to mimic him. Then B mimes the opposite feeling and so on. Continue while there are children willing to be chosen. No one should be coerced into miming.

or

For your eyes only

Grouped in triads, one child should take it in turns to look at the other two. No words, sounds, gestures, or movements of the face are allowed: all feelings are shown only in the eyes. The children being watched should allow themselves to feel the four feelings: happiness, sadness, anger, fear. Initially, the feelings should be done in a set order, for example, glad, sad, angry, scared. After everybody has tried it in this order then they can do it in any order to see if the observer can guess which emotions are being expressed.

The activity can conclude with a group feedback. Generate a discussion by using the following questions: Was it hard to use only your eyes? Do you think that the eyes are a good place to look if you want to know how others are feeling?

What other things do people do which show you how they are feeling (for example, do you tap your feet when you're angry)? Ask the children to demonstrate actions which express feelings.

A vocabulary of feelings

Give the children a sheet of paper and ask them to fold it in four. Ask them to draw one face in each section demonstrating the emotions glad, sad, angry or scared. Then ask the children to list under their drawings as many words as they can, associated with each emotion. They can do this activity during the day, using dictionaries, thesaurus, the Internet perhaps, or ask the family at home to become involved and then share their pictures and words the following day.

Lighthouse

All hold hands and do a Lighthouse. Remind children that the light from a Lighthouse shines in order to help people. It shines in a friendly way, helping everyone that is near it. Ask everyone to look around the circle, make eye contact with some, and smile. This should be a quick activity and done silently. It stops when the hands are parted, which the teacher initiates.

Plan for the day

At the end of each Circle Time (if it's done at the beginning of the day) before anyone gets up, take the opportunity to announce what the plan for the rest of the day will be, to involve the children in the organisation, to remind them of equipment needed and where to find it, to tell them where they need to be at particular times, for example, appointments for doctors or swimming lessons. Wish everyone a happy and productive day. Do the children have any questions or comments?

Circle Time to promote a sense of identity 4

 ### Round

This round will be silent. Using the feelings pictures that were prepared in the previous Circle Time, each child, in turn, will hold up the picture which represents their present feeling. If they are feeling a different emotion and do not have a picture for it, their papers are kept down and their feelings are revealed at the end.

 ### Selection of child

 ### Getting into a tangle

Standing close together, everyone closes their eyes, and on a given signal stretches their arms out and finds a hand to hold. Then, opening their eyes, the children can see if it's possible to unravel the tangle they have created. It is sometimes easier to break into two groups for this activity and certainly if the group is large.

 ### A feeling vocabulary

Begin by asking the children to tell everyone the words they listed next to their feelings pictures. Collectively make a list of these words. These words are important information, as they tell us a lot about each other and how we are at the moment, but you may well be feeling differently before we finish. What makes feelings change?

Then give out a vocabulary of feeling words sheet (page 92). Explain that the bigger the vocabulary we have the better we can understand our feelings and express them clearly to others.

'Pick any three words from your list silently. Now everyone get up and see if you can find two other people who have chosen just one of the words you chose and then sit down together. Sit crosslegged in a close triangle. Choose which of you will be A, B and C.

C can start. C chooses five words from the feeling list. Then, using these words, brainstorm endings to the sentence stems as in this example:

- I feel bored when ...

- I feel left out when ...

- I feel loved when ...

- I feel silly when ...

- I feel annoyed when ...'.

The children should take it in turns, picking five words each time from the list.

Acting

'Now I would like each group to prepare three very short plays or sketches. They can either be performed silently, in mime, or by use of words. This is how you do it. Each person picks a feeling word from the list and thinks of a situation where you have felt like that. Don't tell your group the word. Take it in turns to tell your partners where it was and what happened. Then act the situation in front of them.

'For example, you are at home in a room with your brother and sister. Your brother asks your sister if she would like one of his sweets. She takes one. He does not offer you one. You have to ask him for a sweet, and he then gives you one. How do you think you would feel?

'Another example could be: You and your friends are playing on your bicycles. You fall off your bike and hurt yourself. How do you feel? Act how you feel to the rest of your group.

'When you have all performed your plays in your groups we will get back into the large group and we will guess what each other's emotions are. Remember not to say the word and remember that feelings can usually be seen in the way people act, rather than from what they say.

'Does everyone know what to do?'

Use this opportunity to explain some rudimentary body language. About 60 per cent of communication is non-verbal.

Lighthouse

All hold hands and do a Lighthouse. Remind children that the light from a Lighthouse shines in order to help people. It shines in a friendly way, helping everyone that is near it. Ask everyone to look around the circle, make eye contact with some, and smile. This should be a quick activity and done silently. It stops when the hands are parted, which the teacher initiates.

Plan for the day

At the end of each Circle Time (if it's done at the beginning of the day) before anyone gets up, take the opportunity to announce what the plan for the rest of the day will be, to involve the children in the organisation, to remind them of equipment needed and where to find it, to tell them where they need to be at particular times, for example, appointments for doctors or swimming lessons. Wish everyone a happy and productive day. Do the children have any questions or comments?

Follow-up

Display the vocabulary of feeling words in the classroom and refer to them when any appropriate situation occurs. Tune children in to feelings whenever possible. Make masks representing the four feelings as a craft activity and use them in drama. Plain white ones can be bought and painted.

A vocabulary of feeling words

angry	excited	relaxed
annoyed	fearful	relieved
anxious	flustered	satisfied
apathetic	foolish	scared
bored	frustrated	serious
calm	glad	shocked
cautious	grieved	silly
comfortable	happy	solemn
confident	hesitant	stubborn
confused	hopeful	surprised
contented	jealous	tense
cross	kind	tired
daring	left out	trapped
despairing	lonely	troubled
discontented	loving	uncomfortable
eager	miserable	uneasy
elated	peaceful	warm
embarrassed	pleased	weepy
energetic	proud	wonderful

Can you think of any words to add to this list?

Write them here:

Circle Time to promote a sense of identity 5

 ## Opening round

'I feel great when ... .'

 ## Selection of child

 ## Locomotion

The child who is to have a Special Day can start this game by standing in the centre of the circle and performing any action, for example, waving, and at the same time indicates to three others in the circle to follow on behind, imitating the action.

After they have done so, the last of the four to have been picked points to someone else, who, while the first ones sit down, begins a new action and chooses three others to join in, and so on. The ones who have not had a turn must be picked first. When everyone is sitting, all stand, and it can carry on as before. (Children like this opportunity to show the latest dance steps.)

 ## Groans and gripes

'See if you can find two others with an initial the same as yours, or with the same number of letters in their name as you, and sit down in a triad. Today we will have what I call a gripe time or an opportunity to say what makes you fed up. Take it in turns and complete the sentence: 'The things I don't like doing are...'. You can have as many goes as you want.'

After the triads have had time for a few gripes each, gather the group together for feedback. 'What was it like having a gripe time? Who feels different now? Who can think of ways of dealing with strong feelings?' Generate discussion by asking the group some of the following questions: 'We all know it's good to laugh and smile. Is it all right for boys and men to cry? When is it all right to cry? What happens if you really want to cry but won't let yourself? What else can we do?'

During the discussion try to draw out from children different ways of coping with our emotions, for example, talking to someone, breathing quietly and deeply, writing our thoughts down, hitting things like cushions, even throwing newspaper balls. This can be done by children saying 'When I am cross/unhappy/etc. I can [work out the thing which will help me best and then]...'.

Feelings that are suppressed don't go away and they manifest themselves in our behaviour. Children who are brought up having their feelings constantly denied will first learn to hide their feelings, then learn not to trust their feelings and may eventually learn not to feel. When children are out of touch with their feelings, or suppress their emotions, or are not aware of non-aggressive ways of expressing anger or frustration, conflict invariably surfaces.

> Repressed traumatic experiences in childhood are stored in the body and although remaining unconscious, exert their influence, even in adulthood.
>
> Alice Miller, *The Untouched Key*

Knock knock

See how many jokes people can tell in five minutes.

A chicken crossing the road is poultry in motion.

A boiled egg in the morning is hard to beat.

Visualisation

Guided imagery: The Quick Relax (Chapter 9) or CD sections 4 or 5.

or

 Let everyone enjoy having a long stretch. This can be followed by a jump and shout if desired. Then sit down in the circle.

'Everyone be really quiet, listen to your breathing, close your eyes gently and feel yourself relax from your head to your toes.'

Lighthouse

All hold hands and do a Lighthouse. Remind children that the light from a Lighthouse shines in order to help people. It shines in a friendly way, helping everyone that is near it. Ask everyone to look around the circle, make eye contact with some, and smile. This should be a quick activity and done silently. It stops when the hands are parted, which the teacher initiates.

Plan for the day

At the end of each Circle Time (if it's done at the beginning of the day) before anyone gets up, take the opportunity to announce what the plan for the rest of the day will be, to involve the children in the organisation, to remind them of equipment needed and where to find it, to tell them where they need to be at particular times, for example, appointments for doctors or swimming lessons. Wish everyone a happy and productive day. Do the children have any questions or comments?

Follow-up

Display list of suggested actions made during discussion. Let it be known you are always available to talk with privately if needed. Children could give you a note to ask for this if they did not want others to know. Have a quiet withdrawal area if possible. Arrange for access to a big PE mat to be rolled up and stood up vertically in a corner somewhere. Purchase some sponge rubber fighting sticks.

My name is

_____

This is my picture.

Circle Time to promote a sense of belonging 1

The individual who feels himself understood opens and blossoms out, and even transforms him or herself magically.

Roberto Assagioli, *Psychosynthesis*

 ### Opening round

'The best thing anyone could do for me today would be ... .'

 ### Selection of child

 ### Huggy bear

Children mill around and when a number is called must get into a group of that number and with their arms round each other's shoulders or waists sit in a circle. The last group to sit is out! Continue till one group is left.

I see you

'Today I am going to ask you to find partners like this. Choose any number between one and ten and put that number of fingers up. Then see if you can find two others showing the same number. If you can't, go for the nearest number. Sit in a tight triangle, legs crossed. Name yourselves A, B, C. I want you to take one minute each to describe your partner using the sentence stem: "I see ...". A will start by describing B while C is the observer and has to count the number of things which A says he sees. Use your fingers to keep tally if you like. Here is an example.

'A might look at B and then says: "I see blue eyes, I see bitten nails, I see a smile, I see a tear in a pullover." When he can think of no more, C will tell him how many things he listed. Then change over and everyone gets a turn of speaking, being looked at and counting. See who can make the most descriptions.'

Bring the group together and ask the following questions to generate discussion.

'What was it like describing your partner? When might it be important to describe someone well? Did you describe your partner well? Did he or she think so? Were you pleased with the description of yourself? What did it feel like when you were being described?'

Guess who

Ask a volunteer to describe someone in the room without looking at that person. Then the group will guess who is being described. It is helpful if the teacher demonstrates this.

 ### Circle whisper

Someone whispers a word or phrase into an ear of a neighbour, who then passes it on. This continues round the circle until it returns to the originator who can tell the group if the word or phrase has altered. This is done most successfully by holding hands.

Lighthouse

All hold hands and do a Lighthouse. Remind children that the light from a Lighthouse shines in order to help people. It shines in a friendly way, helping everyone that is near it. Ask everyone to look around the circle, make eye contact with some, and smile. This should be a quick activity and done silently. It stops when the hands are parted, which the teacher initiates.

Plan for the day

At the end of each Circle Time (if it's done at the beginning of the day) before anyone gets up, take the opportunity to announce what the plan for the rest of the day will be, to involve the children in the organisation, to remind them of equipment needed and where to find it, to tell them where they need to be at particular times, for example, appointments for doctors or swimming lessons. Wish everyone a happy and productive day. Do the children have any questions or comments?

Follow-up

Banner: It is good to ask for help when you need to.

Circle Time to promote a sense of belonging 2

 Opening round

'I think a friend is someone who ... .'

 Selection of child

 Group sculptures

Three volunteers go into the middle of the circle and are asked to form an interesting shape together (their bodies must be touching). The rest of the group (in triads) then make up their shapes. Afterwards the triads discuss the shapes they have made. Suggest that the triads try and make several different sculptures. Once everyone is regrouped in the circle, the triads can perform their shapes to the large group.

This activity should end with a whole group sculpture. The Special Day child can start the sculpture by going into the centre of the circle. He then names another child who joins to him in some way. This continues until the whole group, in a multitude of positions, is joined.

It is a good idea to take pictures of this activity. The display of such photos can help the growth of self-esteem.

 I like to hear

Ask the children to look around the circle and count the number of children they have already spoken to today. Ask for examples of what they said to each other.

'Today I'm going to group you into triads by splitting up the circle like cutting a cake.' Go round counting off threes. Make sure each group has paper and a pen or pencil.

'Find a good space for your triad and sit down please. I would like you to write down a list of things you would like to hear people say to you. For example, what would you like to hear from your classmates, your teachers or parents, your brothers and sisters, relatives and shopkeepers?'

Bring the group back together and ask each triad to repeat their lists. Ask for volunteers to make up the lists into a well-decorated book, which can then be displayed as a reminder.

Suggest that from today, and for the rest of the week, they should try to say the things to others that they themselves would like to hear. Next week ask if they did this, and if so, whether they noticed anything different?

†††† Circle squeeze

Standing in a circle, holding hands, a coded message is sent round the circle by a number of short or long but always gentle squeezes. See if the originator receives the same message that he or she sent.

Lighthouse

All hold hands and do a Lighthouse. Remind children that the light from a Lighthouse shines in order to help people. It shines in a friendly way, helping everyone that is near it. Ask everyone to look around the circle, make eye contact with some, and smile. This should be a quick activity and done silently. It stops when the hands are parted, which the teacher initiates.

 Plan for the day

At the end of each Circle Time (if it's done at the beginning of the day) before anyone gets up, take the opportunity to announce what the plan for the rest of the day will be, to involve the children in the organisation, to remind them of equipment needed and where to find it, to tell them where they need to be at particular times, for example, appointments for doctors or swimming lessons. Wish everyone a happy and productive day. Do the children have any questions or comments?

Circle Time to promote a sense of belonging 3

 ### Opening round

'A television advert I like is ... because ... .'

 ### Selection of child

 ### Categories

With the children sitting in a circle, the teacher calls out a category, for example, those whose name begins with A, or those who have a pet. Children to whom this category applies should jump up and sit in the centre of the circle until the next category is called. The game should get faster and faster, ensuring that everyone is included. The last category called should be 'everyone in this room!' When everyone is sitting inside the circle invite the children to have the biggest, longest silent stretch (like a cat) they have ever had, then to go back to their places.

 ### Friends

'I am sure you all see the adverts on television. What do all adverts set out to do? Sell things. Who can name a successful advert? How does it achieve its aim? Who can remember the first friend they ever made? Someone who was not related to you at all, so we won't count cousins, although of course they can be friends as well. Where did you meet this person? What happened? Can you remember who spoke first? Who asked the other to meet again?' Get the children to contribute their experiences.

'Some people have lots of friends and some a few. Both groups are all right. I think most people think friends are important – think of the number of children here who get upset when they break friends. The funny thing is you will never know if someone is going to be a friend until you start talking to them. I always think of meeting a new person as an exciting adventure. It may be the person who is to become your very best friend in all your life. You will never know unless you try.

'I want you to try something now. If I had the power I would now bring into the room a class of children who you didn't know at all – from another planet (not really) – but certainly from another school. I bet you that if I just said "All right, everyone get to know each other", you would very quickly do so. As we can't magic in strangers, we'll do the next best thing. I would like you to think of the children in this class who, for one reason or another, you have not talked to much.'

Pause for the children to consider. 'Now, I'm going to ask you to get into groups with these children, and the way I want you to do it is this. Go up to one person and say "Hello, shall we be in a group?" If you both agree, look round the room and decide between you which other pair you would like to join with, and then ask them.

'When you are a four, sit down, closely together, and tell the others how you felt choosing a partner, and asking, or being asked. See if you can find out if there is a Circle Time game which you all like very much and we will make a list and we can play them, one each day.'

Good friends

'Now I would like you to make a television advert advertising a friend. Discuss and decide on one person in the group who agrees to be advertised as someone you should have as a good friend. Think how you can present them in the best possible way. How can you tell everyone all the good things this person does for others and why she would make a fabulous friend?'

Suggest they make posters, and use music, props and dressing-up clothes. A large cardboard or wooden frame which looks like a television set makes it more realistic. Each group should present its advertisement to the large group. Discuss the merits of each and highlight the good qualities which get shown.

Tell the children about the custom of singing *Auld Lang Syne* and its significance. Let them try, hands crossed, swinging from side to side.

or

Please Mr Policeman, have you seen my friend?

An alternative to the television activity for young children.

One of the children pretends he is lost, walks round the group until he finds the policeman, who has been secretly selected beforehand.

He asks the policeman, 'Please Mr Policemen, have you seen my friend?' The child then goes on to describe his friend to the policeman. For example, 'He phones me if I'm ill', or 'He helps me find lost things'. Do not encourage descriptions of physical characteristics. The policeman guesses who is being described and if he cannot, then he can call in extra help to solve the case. Ensure everyone gets a chance to play all roles eventually.

Lighthouse

All hold hands and do a Lighthouse. Remind children that the light from a Lighthouse shines in order to help people. It shines in a friendly way, helping everyone that is near it. Ask everyone to look around the circle, make eye contact with some, and smile. This should be a quick activity and done silently. It stops when the hands are parted, which the teacher initiates.

Plan for the day

At the end of each Circle Time (if it's done at the beginning of the day) before anyone gets up, take the opportunity to announce what the plan for the rest of the day will be, to involve the children in the organisation, to remind them of equipment needed and where to find it, to tell them where they need to be at particular times, for example, appointments for doctors or swimming lessons. Wish everyone a happy and productive day. Do the children have any questions or comments?

Circle Time to promote a sense of belonging 4

 ## Opening round

Hold up a sign 'Co-operation is ... .'

'We are going to explore the meaning of the word co-operation today, and see what we can discover about it and what it means to us. As the sheet comes to you, hold it up to the group and finish the sentence.'

Examples are:

Co-operation is to volunteer to do something in the group

Co-operation is to wait your turn

Co-operation is to be friendly

Co-operation is to listen

Co-operation is sharing with others.

 ## Selection of child

 ## Fruit salad

Give each child a name of a fruit – apple, banana, pear, orange – and repeat round the circle. Then call out one fruit and those who have the name of that fruit change places with each other. The last one seated is out. If you call 'fruit salad' everyone moves. Let the children volunteer to do the calling.

 ## Co-operation

Ask the children to mill around the room. When they are well mixed ask them to close their eyes and gently find two others. Then ask the triads to prepare a playlet or sketch, which is a good example of children, or grown-ups, co-operating. Each triad should act their sketch to the large group.

 ## Decisions

'Join your triad to another triad. Now imagine one of you has a birthday coming and you are all going to the party. It can either be held at home or, for example, McDonald's or the Happy Eater, or somewhere else. In your group, brainstorm all the reasons for and against where to hold it and decide which venue you would prefer'. Each group then presents their reasons to the big group who will take a vote.

Tell the group they can have a party in school one day this week if they will arrange it themselves as a practical example of co-operation.

Lighthouse. Shine a smile round the group

Plan for the day

At the end of each Circle Time (if it's done at the beginning of the day) before anyone gets up, take the opportunity to announce what the plan for the rest of the day will be, to involve the children in the organisation, to remind them of equipment needed and where to find it, to tell them where they need to be at particular times, for example, appointments for doctors or swimming lessons. Wish everyone a happy and productive day. Do the children have any questions or comments?

Circle Time to promote a sense of belonging 5

 ### Opening round

'I was helped once when someone ... .'

 ### Selection of child

 ### People machines

Ask for three volunteers and then ask if they can think of a way to pretend to be a washing machine. Show two of them how to hold hands with outstretched arms while the third pretends to tumble around inside as the laundry. Group the others into triads. Ask them to make a machine, for example, a car, typewriter or computer. Then each triad should demonstrate their inventions to the rest of the group.

 ### Insults

Ask the children to find two partners who like the same desserts as they do, for example, yoghurt, rice pudding or apple tart. Give each triad two large sheets of paper.

'Now the other day we were thinking of things we like to hear people say to us. Today I would like us to spend time thinking about the opposite – the things we don't like to hear. Perhaps you have a name for statements like these. Any suggestions? Put-down is one, sarcasm or insult are others. They are really nasty and they hurt even though no one hits or punches. Make a list, now, of as many horrible things you don't want to hear as you can think of.'

After a suitable time ask them to underline the three which they think are the worst, and then read them out to the big group.

 ### Nasty moments

'Now, in your triads decide who will be A, B and C. Take one minute each and tell the others of a time, an experience, when you had a put-down from someone and how it felt. On the second sheet I gave you make a list of as many feelings as you can remember which you had when it happened.'

Bring the groups back to the circle and ask the children which feelings they recorded.

 ### Goodbye to put-downs

'I would like to ask you an important question. Would it be possible to create an environment in this room where there are no put-downs? How many would like to see this happen in here? Put up your hands if you would. In that case I suggest we have a ceremony to get rid of the put-downs.'

Tear the put-downs listed on the first sheets into separate statements, then put them all into a prepared box – a shoe box or breakfast cereal box, coloured, or covered in black, and then if possible find somewhere convenient outside where the group can go to bury the box. Alternatively it can be burnt. Get children to arrange a ceremony they think appropriate.

Rejecting put-downs

If someone forgets, and attempts to use any put-downs, I suggest you remind them by telling them something like this: 'I feel that what you are saying is a put-down and I'd like to remind you that dead words have no life in this classroom.' Another way, if you don't want to say all that, is to put two fingers in a V and make a noise like a snake, a hissing sound, to tell them that you recognise a put-down, to go away or 'I do not like what you are saying to me. I would prefer you to be a friend.'

No Matter What You Say or Do To Me

I Am Still A Worthwhile Person

Lighthouse

All hold hands and do a Lighthouse. Remind children that the light from a Lighthouse shines in order to help people. It shines in a friendly way, helping everyone that is near it. Ask everyone to look around the circle, make eye contact with some, and smile. This should be a quick activity and done silently. It stops when the hands are parted, which the teacher initiates.

Plan for the day

At the end of each Circle Time (if it's done at the beginning of the day) before anyone gets up, take the opportunity to announce what the plan for the rest of the day will be, to involve the children in the organisation, to remind them of equipment needed and where to find it, to tell them where they need to be at particular times, for example, appointments for doctors or swimming lessons. Wish everyone a happy and productive day. Do the children have any questions or comments?

Follow-up

Read *IALAC (I Am Lovable and Capable)* The story of 14-year-old Randy whose IALAC sign got destroyed during the day. Everyone needs to hear this. Re-enact it.

Badge for Belonging.

Willpower is...

Circle Time to promote a sense of purpose 1

The nice thing about mistakes is that they don't have to be permanent.

Spencer Tracy, in the film *Edison – the Man* about Thomas Alvar Edison. Edison
made 9000 attempts before he succeeded in making a light bulb work.

 ### Opening round

'Good morning everyone. If I have the chance today I would like to... .'

 ### Selection of child

 ### The power game (1)

The aim of these simple games is to get across the message that goals can be achieved
through determination and being prepared to learn to concentrate. It would depend
on the ages of the children involved, but usually I delay any explanation until a
discussion on goal-setting takes place and treat it purely as a fun activity.

The adult demonstrates by standing and then saying, for example, 'I will tap my
left foot with my right thumb four times', and doing so. All the children are asked
to stand and to copy. It is essential that everyone says the statement before the
action. The use of the words 'I will' is crucial. Other examples are: 'I will clap my
hands six times,' 'I will pat my head with my left hand for eight counts.'

The level of complication of instruction depends on the age of the children, as does
the decision to count out loud.

Ask for volunteers to choose the activity. A helpful rule is not to allow activities
which involve touching others. Tell the children that there are times when it is
important to know what others are doing, and times when it is not. Make sure
everyone is saying the 'I will' statement and note the difference it makes.

 Begin the discussion by asking the children which games they like to play, then elicit
answers to the following questions. 'Which of the games you have mentioned are
played with other people? If it is a game involving more than one against one, what
do you call members of a group playing against another group? Do you enjoy being
a member of a team? What makes a good team? What does each member need to do
to be a good team member? What are the ways each member can help the others?'

 ### Encouraging others

'Now, so that everyone gets more talking time I'm going to ask you to form triads.
I would like you to choose two others who like playing the same games as you, any
games from football and netball to board games like Scrabble or snakes and ladders.
When you have done so, sit together in a close triangle. Each triad needs a piece of
paper and something to write with.

'Are you settled? Good. I would like you to imagine now that you have just been appointed the manager of a professional team. It doesn't matter what the game is, because the managers all have the same basic role – to look after the team and encourage it to win. They do this in a number of ways; they see how much the players are paid, they look after their health and try to keep them fit by employing doctors and others, they try to improve their skills by getting them to practise and using coaches to help them. Above all else they need to get players to believe in themselves that they are good players and have the ability to win. What would you say to the players before a game, at half time, at the end? Remember they have another game to play soon. For example, she or he might say "Great work, keep it up", or "I saw you try really hard". Talk about and make a list of all the useful phrases you can think of which would encourage your players to be a good team.'

After an appropriate time ask the children to return to the whole group and share their suggestions. Write these on a large sheet for display.

 ## Encouraging ourselves

'When else is it good to make comments like this? Who else can they be said to?' Family and friends will be the most likely answers. Repeat the question and persist with it to see if someone will say 'To yourself'. If so, praise, pointing to appropriate phrases on the list. If not, tell the children that while it's really pleasant to hear other people saying things like these to you, the best person to say them to is yourself.

'Why is that? Other people who will do this may not always be around when you need them; sometimes people say these things and you don't always believe them. You are always there, and you should always be able to believe yourself.

'Pick a phrase from the list, the one you like best. Say it to yourself.' Here modelling helps tremendously and the adult should pick a phrase and say it aloud. Ask for volunteers to share their favourite, get everyone to say theirs aloud at the same time.

'Everyone think of a time when you have had something hard to do, like learning new maths or spellings perhaps, or something you have not wanted to do, like cleaning up an untidy bedroom. Can you picture the scene? When you can, say your phrase, for example, "You can do it" and then see yourself succeeding, winning.

'This is called self-talk. We all talk to ourselves all the time, although we often don't realise it. Does anyone know of things they say to themselves? It's very easy to say things to ourselves which are not helpful and do not encourage us – things like "That was silly" or "You are an idiot". If you catch yourself saying them, say, "Hey, that's not right, I'm OK", or something similar. Remember, if we want ourselves to win, we must do the same.

'The list we have made consists of positive statements. We need to say them to ourselves all the time. If you think any negative thoughts, change them to positive thoughts and you are much more likely to win at whatever you are doing.

'Each day from now on I am going to spare some time for people to share their experiences, to tell us what happens when they use positive thoughts to help them achieve something. So I am going to look forward to hearing yours.'

Visualisation

Guided imagery: My Best Friend on CD is appropriate here. Read instructions in Chapter 9 first.

Lighthouse

All hold hands and do a Lighthouse. Remind children that the light from a Lighthouse shines in order to help people. It shines in a friendly way, helping everyone that is near it. Ask everyone to look around the circle, make eye contact with some, and smile. This should be a quick activity and done silently. It stops when the hands are parted, which the teacher initiates.

Plan for the day

At the end of each Circle Time (if it's done at the beginning of the day) before anyone gets up, take the opportunity to announce what the plan for the rest of the day will be, to involve the children in the organisation, to remind them of equipment needed and where to find it, to tell them where they need to be at particular times, for example, appointments for doctors or swimming lessons. Wish everyone a happy and productive day. Do the children have any questions or comments?

Follow-up

Have a list of positive phrases prominently on display for them to use.

To be a winner say:

> I'm sure you can handle it
>
> Well done
>
> I like the way you did that
>
> Just take one step at a time
>
> I have confidence in myself
>
> You can do it
>
> That's a good try
>
> You'll get there
>
> Try looking at it in a different way
>
> Everyone makes mistakes and that's OK
>
> Have another go
>
> That's a really good, wonderful, lovely …
>
> That's an excellent …
>
> That's skilful, brilliant, fantastic …

Banner: It's fine to make mistakes. That's the way we learn.

Circle Time to promote a sense of purpose 2

 ## Opening round 1

'If I could have things just as I want them … .'

 ## Selection of child

The power game (2)

This is a variation on power game 1. Three volunteers go to the centre of the circle, silently decide on the activities they are going to do, and then on a given signal announce them, using an 'I will' statement, and then execute them simultaneously. The aim is not to be distracted by what the other two are doing and to complete the task without hesitation. Children who do so can be called 'Winners'.

The game can be made easier or harder by:

a)   varying the number of children in the centre

b)   insisting the contestants stand facing each other

c)   changing the number of activities to be performed, for example, 'I will clap once, jump three times and hop twice'.

Encourage those that have difficulty. End by having everyone doing it together.

Winners

'If you hear someone described as a winner what do you know about them? What do you have to do to be a winner? Can only adults be winners? Winners are those people who succeed in what they set out to do.' Tell the group about the annual Children of Courage awards given to children who have overcome their handicaps, illnesses or accidents by bravery, determination and persistence. There may be children in the group with similar experiences or they may know someone else who has.

'Do you have to have a handicap etc. before you can become a winner?' Tell the children about Edison's determination to invent an electric light bulb, about Hillary's ascent of Everest, Bannister's attack on the four-minute mile and ask the children if they know of other examples.

Ask the children if they have read any fiction about children or adults who were winners, for example, Dahl's *Danny Champion of the World*, Forrest Wilson's *Supergran*.

'The game we played is called Power Game. Power drives things; we get power from wind, nuclear energy, coal, etc. Where do people get their power from? We call it willpower.'

Round

Hold up a sign with 'Willpower is …' on it. 'Let's have a good think about willpower because it's very important for all of us. Let us try to describe it in other words so that we can get a really good idea of what it means.'

The teacher starts by completing the phrase and then moving round the circle in turn, everyone completes the phrase in their own way. Passes should be allowed, but children who do should be invited to contribute at the end, as it is often the case that they only want more thinking time.

Examples are: Willpower is keeping going; willpower is stickability; willpower is being determined; willpower is not giving up; willpower is feeling strong; willpower is being able to concentrate.

People you know

'Form triads now please. Today find two partners who have got the same size, or very nearly, hand span as yours.' When the children are settled give them a choice in the way they tackle this activity.

'Please think of people you know or have heard about who you would call winners. They can be people in your family, perhaps a grandparent or cousin, or someone you have read about or seen on television who you would describe as a winner. Talk about them and what happened and then decide on one person you would like to tell the group about. You can do that in one of three ways. You can tell us about her, name who she was, what she did, where it happened, or draw a picture to show those things or mime what happened. I hope you will be able to agree on how to present it to the group. Any questions? You have ten minutes to prepare.'

Return to the whole group and share the presentations. Remind the children about the value of positive statements. Ask them to guess which phrases these winners used.

What I have done

An alternative, or additional activity, is to ask the children to make up a chart recording all the positive events in their lives. Reference to parents might be necessary for some of the information. The smallest success is worth recording; it might be very significant to the child. Every attempt, every risk at some new activity which succeeds is important to the person that does it. Children like the opportunity to present these artistically in a variety of ways.

Mary Brown

Date	Event	Date	Event
	born		rode a bicycle
	cut first tooth		won a prize at the fair
	said 'dada'		got a swimming certificate
	walked		joined a judo club
	started nursery		slept in a tent

Lighthouse

All hold hands and do a Lighthouse. Remind children that the light from a Lighthouse shines in order to help people. It shines in a friendly way, helping everyone that is near it. Ask everyone to look around the circle, make eye contact with some, and smile. This should be a quick activity and done silently. It stops when the hands are parted, which the teacher initiates.

Plan for the day

At the end of each Circle Time (if it's done at the beginning of the day) before anyone gets up, take the opportunity to announce what the plan for the rest of the day will be, to involve the children in the organisation, to remind them of equipment needed and where to find it, to tell them where they need to be at particular times, for example, appointments for doctors or swimming lessons. Wish everyone a happy and productive day. Do the children have any questions or comments?

Follow-up

Willpower illustration is for a) sentence completions, b) record past achievements, or c) list more targets.

Read *The 18th Emergency* by Betsy Byers, published in 1973 and in print ever since. The school bully is out to get Mouse Fawley and while Mouse is waiting he thinks of 17 other emergencies (lion attack, appearance of shark, strangulation by boa constrictor) all of which he can handle. Hysterically funny.

> Each human being is born as something new, something that never existed before. He is born with what he needs to win at life. Each can be significant, thinking, aware and creatively productive in his own right – a winner.
>
> M. James and D. Jongward, *Born to Win*

Circle Time to promote a sense of purpose 3

Opening round

'I would like to help to ... .'

Selection of child

The power game (3)

Several volunteers go to the centre of the circle, make an 'I will' statement and perform their activities all together, as in power game 2.

Now, however, time is introduced, test them to see if they can keep going for 30 seconds. After several turns this can be altered so the children do not know the time limit and have to wait for the adult's signal. They lose if they stop before time; those that keep going are winners.

Another variation is when a 'fool' is introduced, a child who will dance around, make faces and try to distract the others.

My goals

'Do you know how to stretch? Winners know how to stretch. They aim for things which are just within their reach if they use their willpower. Just like teams use all their willpower to win their games, so do winners use all their strength to achieve their aims. Their aims are things they want to do, they go for a goal or a target.

'Today I would like you to think of some goals you would like to achieve, not big ones which you will do when you grow up, but small goals you can do today. Think of some things that you don't usually do that you would like to have done before bedtime tonight. Or perhaps something you would like to be better at doing or perhaps something you have never done and would like to try for the first time.

'Let's think of some examples. One might be where your teacher has often suggested that stories you write be longer. Today you can use your willpower to write half a page more than last time you wrote.

'Perhaps your locker is always untidy and you take a long time to find things. Today is the day when it will be put straight. Or would you like to be a neater writer? The way to tackle that big goal would be to choose just one letter that is not as good as it could be and really concentrate on improving it.

'It could be a physical skill you want to aim at – perhaps ten more skips than you usually do, five minutes longer at shooting at goal, seeing how fast you can become dribbling round skittles. The best sports people today started by setting small targets and going up one step at a time – some as far as the steps to the dais to get their Olympic medals.

'I would like you to think of some goals you can achieve outside school, for example, cleaning your teeth before you are asked to do it, helping to look after a younger brother or sister by playing a game with him or her, making your parents a cup of tea. What you choose should be something which would be good to do, and if you use your willpower, possible for you to do.

'Find now please two partners who are exactly or very nearly the same height as you, and sit comfortably close together so you can easily hear each other talk. Everyone needs a paper and pencil. Decide who will be A, B and C. A will go first and tell B and C what her goals are – make a list of at least five. B and C are to share writing them down. When you have done that, put them in number order, so you decide which one you will do first.

'B and C have turns at making a list of goals, then I want you to have your own sheets and write down next to each goal the name of anyone who you might want to help you in some way get that goal, to give you some advice perhaps or give you some equipment so that you can do it. It might be a friend, teacher, or relative. This person might also be the person you would like to tell when you have achieved your goal.

'Finally I would like you to write at the bottom of the sheet anything you think may stop you from winning. I could suggest that perhaps you will not give yourself time to do it properly, or you might forget. You might even decide you are too lazy to do it.' Ask for examples. 'This is called personal sabotage.'

Bring the children back to the whole group. Ask if everyone understands. The aim is for everyone to do at least one task on their sheet today. Tell them winners start today, don't delay. Remind them to give themselves some good self-talk.

Lighthouse

All hold hands and do a Lighthouse. Remind children that the light from a Lighthouse shines in order to help people. It shines in a friendly way, helping everyone that is near it. Ask everyone to look around the circle, make eye contact with some, and smile. This should be a quick activity and done silently. It stops when the hands are parted, which the teacher initiates.

Plan for the day

At the end of each Circle Time (if it's done at the beginning of the day) before anyone gets up, take the opportunity to announce what the plan for the rest of the day will be, to involve the children in the organisation, to remind them of equipment needed and where to find it, to tell them where they need to be at particular times, for example, appointments for doctors or swimming lessons. Wish everyone a happy and productive day. Do the children have any questions or comments?

Circle Time to promote a sense of purpose (4)

 ### Opening round

'Something I wish I ... .'

 ### Selection of child

 ### Zoom zoom

In a seated circle the leader begins by making a humming noise like the sound of a racing car. The next person joins in and so on round the circle several times. Then change to the hum just passing round to only one person at a time. Anyone has the power to reverse the car as when the hum gets to them they do not look to the right but back at the existing hummer and so it goes back the other way. With the car going backwards and forwards it can be a fast game. A second car can be introduced which must not collide with the first.

 ### The power game (4)

The aim of this activity is to demonstrate to the children how choices are made and the power of decision.

'In a moment I'm going to ask everyone to get up and go and do something. What that something is I'm going to leave completely up to you. The only rules are that it must be done inside the room, not hurt anybody or damage property. Just have a look around and think of all the possibilities that are open to you.' (Only give examples if the children are very young.)

'I'm going to count to three and when I get to three I want you all to get up and do whatever you are going to do and then in one minute come back and sit in the circle.'

Repeat several times. Observe those children who do this confidently without the need to copy others.

'Now I'm going to ask you to do it again. Have you decided what you will do this time? I shall count 1, 2, stop. See if you can change your mind quickly. Don't do what you were going to do, do something else instead as quickly as you can, now.' Watch for children's reactions and how quickly they move.

'This is the last time. Ready? Have you decided what you would like to do? Now this one also has a little twist in it. When I count 3, I would like you to get up, go to wherever you were going and then decide not to do it and come back and sit down instead. Remember, this is not me telling you not to do something, but you changing your mind and seeing how that feels. Ready, 1, 2, 3.

 'I expect you have all heard the story of Aladdin and his magic lamp. In the lamp was a genie that would pop out and grant any wish. Sometimes you see on television programmes where people get surprised and they have their wishes come true for them. Has anyone ever had a wish come true?'

Encourage children to share; self-disclose something of your own.

'Everyone has wishes and dreams. It is fine to have them. What we need to do is to see the difference between those that we can make happen and those we cannot. A boy told me once he hated the freckles on his face and so wished to get rid of them. No one has ever thought of a way of doing that, even though science and medicine can do wonderful things. He did actually look fine but he did not think so and wanted to get rid of them. There are some things that are a waste of time and energy to wish for because they can never happen. It's more sensible to put all your effort into working to make those wishes that can happen actually come true.'

Wishes

'Today I'm going to ask you to be by yourselves for a little while. Take a piece of paper and find somewhere quiet to sit on your own. On the paper draw a line down the middle and then on one side put down anything that you think you might like to wish for which you know can never be, and on the other wishes that could come true. They can be wishes for today, or something which you would like to happen in the future, perhaps when you are grown up. They do not have to involve having a lot of money. You may draw pictures instead of using words if you wish.'

After a set period tell the children how long they will have and let them know when there is two minutes left to finish. Bring them back to the whole group and ask them to share.

Be prepared for some personal disclosures and the feelings which accompany them. Stay with the wishes that can be accomplished. Once wishes are expressed and recognised as normal, they are likely to motivate children into action. With emphasis on goal-setting, children who have a history of failure and seem scripted for defeat, begin to realise that by the use of the will, some wishes may be attained. It becomes self-perpetuating and leads to more and more success.

Take one or two samples and, by questioning the whole group, put together a plan for the child to show how the wish can be attained. Make an action plan showing the small steps which will eventually lead to success. Follow-up work is highly desirable, giving time and help to the child to see that she is getting enough support. Remind her to use her favourite positive statements, to write them down, and say them aloud and to share her aims with others. If the opportunity can be given to help each child who has declared a realistic wish, the benefits will be both immediate and far reaching.

 ## An alternative activity

'Find two others who have the same/opposite colour eyes, and, taking turns, A, B and C have three minutes each to complete this round: "If I had all the money I wanted the things I would do for myself would be … and for other people would be … ." '

In the whole group encourage free discussion. 'Did your partners have some good ideas? Any you would do too? Were there any surprises? How important is money?'

Visualisation

Guided imagery: The Magic Island on CD. Read Chapter 9 first.

Lighthouse

All hold hands and do a Lighthouse. Remind children that the light from a Lighthouse shines in order to help people. It shines in a friendly way, helping everyone that is near it. Ask everyone to look around the circle, make eye contact with some, and smile. This should be a quick activity and done silently. It stops when the hands are parted, which the teacher initiates.

Plan for the day

At the end of each Circle Time (if it's done at the beginning of the day) before anyone gets up, take the opportunity to announce what the plan for the rest of the day will be, to involve the children in the organisation, to remind them of equipment needed and where to find it, to tell them where they need to be at particular times, for example, appointments for doctors or swimming lessons. Wish everyone a happy and productive day. Do the children have any questions or comments?

Circle Time to promote a sense of purpose (5)

Opening round

'I am looking forward to …' or 'I like to enjoy myself by … .'

Selection of child

The power game (5)

This is best played standing to allow for more variety of movement. The adult begins by making a sound and an action at the same time, e.g. stamping on leg, waving and saying 'Hurray'. As soon as the child on her left sees what it is, she copies, then the next child copies her and so on round the circle, each copying the person on the left, until everyone is doing it. After a few seconds the child on the left of the adult begins a new sound and movement which gets copied in a similar fashion. No one ends one movement until she has a new one to copy from the left. The children become very inventive with their sounds and movement. It gives them an opportunity in a very simple way to make a decision which affects others.

Thunderstorm

An enjoyable variation is when the group, through sound and movement, simulate a thunderstorm. The leader begins each movement which is then copied round the circle as before. It begins very quietly, reaches a crescendo, then gradually dies away. The sequence is: a) palms rubbed together, b) one finger tapping a palm, then two three, four fingers in turn, c) slow handclaps, d) loud handclaps, e) handclaps and foot tapping, f) fast claps and stamping, g) then reverse the order. Other stories in mime can be told in this way.

Group goals

'We have been talking about goals and targets that each of you has set for yourselves. Today I would like us to think of a goal we can aim at all together. Like the game we have just played, we shall all have to be in unison if we are to be successful. What could we choose? What would give us all a good feeling if it was accomplished by everyone? What is the burning issue in this group?' Ask for ideas, brainstorm, list them and do not comment – if a teacher says 'Good' about one idea and nothing about another, it not only influences children's opinions but inhibits further suggestions.

Discuss them, consider ways that all opinions can be respected and arrive at a truly democratic decision. The goal is more likely to be successful if chosen in this manner. Success in achieving one goal will lead to more being set and accomplished. Bring up the question of ways to help children who may find it difficult.

Are there any practical solutions, e.g. reminders from friends? Point out the difference between gentle encouragement and nagging – which do they prefer? Remind them of expressions that are used to help team members. Finally, tell them that each one of us is responsible for our own actions. We all need support, but as long as the goal is realistic and achievable then we will expect everyone else to do their bit and to win! The goal should be measurable and specific, e.g., everyone to be punctual; everyone to have PE/games kit when required; only fuzzies and compliments to be used about others' work or behaviour; a piece of work set is completed.

Other people's achievements

An additional or alternative activity:

'Choose two partners who have the same size hands as you. Sit in a triad. On a piece of paper make a list of as many different activities which you can think of which you know other girls and boys have chosen to do but which you have never done.' Examples are: learnt to juggle, grown flowers, made a den, stamp collecting.

After the required time return to the whole group. Make a list and leave on display. Children who have done any of the activities should be identified, perhaps listed if they are willing to help or advise anyone else who would like to try how to start. Encouraging children to discover strengths like these in home, holiday, after-school activities leads to more self-esteem and higher academic achievement.

Visualisation

Guided imagery: The Road To Success on CD. Read Chapter 9 first.

Lighthouse

All hold hands and do a Lighthouse. Remind children that the light from a Lighthouse shines in order to help people. It shines in a friendly way, helping everyone that is near it. Ask everyone to look around the circle, make eye contact with some, and smile. This should be a quick activity and done silently. It stops when the hands are parted, which the teacher initiates.

Plan for the day

At the end of each Circle Time (if it's done at the beginning of the day) before anyone gets up, take the opportunity to announce what the plan for the rest of the day will be, to involve the children in the organisation, to remind them of equipment needed and where to find it, to tell them where they need to be at particular times, for example, appointments for doctors or swimming lessons. Wish everyone a happy and productive day. Do the children have any questions or comments?

Follow-up

Badge: Purpose: I shall do it.

Read *The Warm Fuzzy Tale* by Steiner and discover wonderful warm fuzzies and cold pricklies. Tell the story, re-enact it.

To the top

Name: _____

When I get to the top I will have

Circle Time to promote a sense of competence 1

How would you like to be remembered?

As someone who did the best she could with the talents she had.

J.K. Rowling, author of *Harry Potter*, in a television interview December 2007

Opening round

'It was hard to do but finally I … .'

Selection of child

The car wash

Remind the children of the purpose of a car wash. The owner of the vehicle wants the vehicle to look at its best. The oil and petrol and servicing can be compared to the diet it needs, the car wash to make it clean and sparkling.

Ask the group to form two lines facing each other, close together. A volunteer stands at the top between the two lines facing the group. She puts the magic coin in the machine and enters the car wash, moving slowly and bending forward. As she goes through hands come from everywhere to stroke, rub, polish the head, shoulders, arms, legs and feet giving a real shine for the day.

Encourage gentle but firm strokes. Let all who wish to have a turn. This is a very popular activity. I strongly recommend that a car wash is offered to the Special Day child every day – it doesn't take a minute, although some other children usually manage to slip through as well – and is such a worthwhile experience. Many children (and adults) do not get the amount of touch they need for growth; this is a friendly, harmless way to give some. The car comes out smiling and ready to perform well!

Tunnels

An alternative, more robust version, known as 'tunnels', can be used where the lines stand almost touching. No arms or hands can be used and the volunteer, either upright or on hands and knees, has to push her way through the tunnel. I have witnessed some children who are usually very withdrawn welcome the opportunity to do this.

Boasting vs pride

Ask the children what bragging and boasting means. Is it like lying? Why do people do it? Refer to the adventures of Baron Munchausen. Do they know anyone like that?

'I think it is important to know what bragging feels like, so I suggest we all have a turn. It is fine to do it when it's a fun activity like this. Let me give you an example:

'I play the guitar. I am the best guitar player in the world. When I play, everyone in the street outside stops to listen. I was not taught, but could play when I was very young, before I could walk ...', etc., etc. Really exaggerate so that children get the idea of how extreme it can be.

'Now I would like you to choose two partners who you think are good at telling stories and sit in a group with them. Choose A, B, C, so you know in which order you are going to speak. Bragging is not quite the same as lying. I would have been lying if I said I could play the guitar but couldn't. Bragging is about being able to play the guitar, and then claiming to be better than absolutely everyone else. Even the best football player in the world does not win all his matches. Take turns and take about a minute each to tell your partners about something you do well, perhaps a hobby you have or something you've learned at school, and boast about it for all you are worth.'

After they have done that, say 'I would like you to try something else now. Have another round, talk about the same topic and tell your partners how good you are, something which makes you feel good doing, but without bragging. I want to encourage you to say things like "I do it well", "I am good at it,", "I know how to do it", "I m pleased with what I do". Don't be shy, this is not bragging. Your partners can help you if you dry up by saying "Tell us more". They will want to know everything you do. Have more than one topic if you want to.

'When each person finishes I would like the other two of you to say to her "Thank you for telling us that, it sounds as if you do it well", or something similar. It should sound the same to the person as having a nice pat on the back would feel.'

Return to the big group for summing up. Ask the children if they could see the difference between the first and second rounds. Did their feelings change? Were they uncomfortable bragging, or listening to others brag? What about the second round?

Explain that bragging is usually caused by not feeling very sure about yourself, so you try to make up for this by claiming to be better than others. People who do this need friends who will help them feel all right. Emphasise that talking about ourselves and our ideas is important and is not bragging. When we can speak positively about ourselves, it helps us to learn, get on with other people and be happy.

Encourage the children to practise doing it during the day whenever they have an opportunity. Provide time for a check-up/feedback at the next session.

Lighthouse

All hold hands and do a Lighthouse. Remind children that the light from a Lighthouse shines in order to help people. It shines in a friendly way, helping everyone that is near it. Ask everyone to look around the circle, make eye contact with some, and smile. This should be a quick activity and done silently. It stops when the hands are parted, which the teacher initiates.

Plan for the day

At the end of each Circle Time (if it's done at the beginning of the day) before anyone gets up, take the opportunity to announce what the plan for the rest of the day will be, to involve the children in the organisation, to remind them of equipment needed and where to find it, to tell them where they need to be at particular times, for example, appointments for doctors or swimming lessons. Wish everyone a happy and productive day. Do the children have any questions or comments?

Follow-up

Banner: If it's a sensible risk go for it and get it.

The Surprising Adventures of Baron Munchausen, 1720–1797. According to the stories related to others the Baron's astonishing adventures included riding on cannonballs, travelling to the moon and escaping from a swamp by pulling himself up by his own hair. Most of the stories were based on folk tales.

Circle Time to promote a sense of competence 2

Opening round

'Good morning. I want you to know that I know how to ... .'

Selection of child

Name game

Each child is to think of something they consider themselves good at or a quality which they believe themselves to have or are developing – something which they are pleased to draw to the attention of the group. Give time for children to choose. Children who need a prompt can ask friends. The teacher can make suggestions. Then the round begins and the children prefix their name with the word chosen, for example, 'I am mathematical John', 'I'am punctual Sarah'. At the end of the round children can be invited to see if they can remember the description used by others.

A circle of appreciation

These descriptions can be helpful when holding an appreciations circle. This can happen at any time, especially when it is not convenient to give a Special Day to one child, or at the beginning of a new term or the end of a year, or when the class has accomplished something by working together.

Each child in turn receives the compliments and appreciations of others in the group. The remarks should be as specific as possible, for example, 'I liked it when ...' and opinions always prefaced by 'I think ...', 'I believe ...', etc. Adults can remind children that appreciations should be for what people are as well as what they do, for example, 'I'm glad you are in this class', 'I am pleased to share this time with you.'

Recorded compliments

If the opportunity can be given for these remarks to be written down so much the better. Sometimes children can be asked to circulate, writing their compliments on others' sheets of paper. The time given to this activity is well spent. Research shows that children who give compliments to others greatly increase their own self-esteem while doing so.

Interviews

Now give out paper and ask the children to prepare for a television or radio interview. A reporter has got in touch to say that she is coming to interview them and in order to save time and so that they will have the opportunity to say what they want to say about themselves, she would like them each to prepare five questions which she can use when interviewing. Remind them that it is not bragging to speak positively about themselves. Help them to frame the questions. They can be about their best features, successes in the past – a piece of school work they are proud of – something they liked finding out about, somewhere they have been, something they have done for others.

- What are you good at?

- What have you learnt to do recently?

- What would your best friend say about it?

- Name some good deeds you have done.

- What do you like to be called?

- When do you feel at your best?

- Talk about a hobby or game you like.

The reason for the interview can be some special occasion in school, or a more far-fetched one, such as publicity for a proposed rocket trip. When the questions are ready, choose to have the children sit in small groups or the big group, whichever is appropriate, and take turns to be interviewed by the others. Recording equipment adds realism.

Skills for success

An alternative activity is to think of five compliments beginning with the words 'I am …' and to get them to think of what they are rather than what they do. If a child says 'I am a good footballer', ask him what qualities he has to have to be that – co-operative, quick thinking, etc. Give lots of examples.

Success diaries

This exercise can be used for the introduction of success diaries. Children who have the opportunity to record successes remember these when they are about to embark on another piece of learning, or new behaviour, and they are a great morale-booster and confidence-builder. The books can be a source of pride for years to come. They are good items to be able to produce when starting a new school, or to show to grandparents.

Visualisation

Guided Imagery: Dancing On A Rainbow on CD. Read Chapter 9 first.

Lighthouse

All hold hands and do a Lighthouse. Remind children that the light from a Lighthouse shines in order to help people. It shines in a friendly way, helping everyone that is near it. Ask everyone to look around the circle, make eye contact with some, and smile. This should be a quick activity and done silently. It stops when the hands are parted, which the teacher initiates.

Plan for the day

At the end of each Circle Time (if it's done at the beginning of the day) before anyone gets up, take the opportunity to announce what the plan for the rest of the day will be, to involve the children in the organisation, to remind them of equipment needed and where to find it, to tell them where they need to be at particular times, for example, appointments for doctors or swimming lessons. Wish everyone a happy and productive day. Do the children have any questions or comments?

Circle Time to promote a sense of competence 3

 Opening round

'This week I am especially interested in … .'

 Selection of child

 Decisions

'Today I am going to ask you to make lots of decisions. To start, there is a choice of activity. You can either choose to have a noisy time by having a jump and a yell, or a quieter time by sitting upright and concentrating on your breathing with your eyes closed. Those people who want to do the first show your hands; the second activity show yours. Now get into position where you will disturb no one else, and then you have one minute to do what you have chosen before returning to the circle.'

 Inventions

'The next thing I would like you to do is to choose two partners and find a space to sit in.' When they are ready to proceed, say 'I have asked you to make people machines before. Today I am going to ask you to do this again with a slight difference. I want you to think of an invention which has become one of the top ten most useful machines in the world. When you have picked one, use your bodies and any equipment we have here to show it working in some way. Then when you have practised it to your satisfaction find another triad to demonstrate it to. If those boys and girls can guess what it is, give yourselves a pat on the back. Is that clear? Any questions? Start when you are ready. You have 15 minutes to do everything before I shall ask you to return to the circle.' Be sensitive to the needs of children when forming the triads but hold back from making suggestions or giving help unless absolutely necessary.

 Easy or difficult?

'So what was that like? What a lot of decisions I asked you to make. First, finding partners. Did you do the asking or did you wait to be asked? Who decided which machine you would make? How many suggestions did you have to choose from? How did you choose which other triad to ask to see your machine?'

Allow time for children to respond to the questions, and be ready to encourage any who may feel anxious about contributing. 'How many decisions have you made already today? What were they? For example, when to get up, what to eat, wear, which way to come to school, who to talk to when you got here. Do you think you can live without making decisions? Only if you let other people make them for you. Would you want that? It would mean other people telling you what to do all the time – which books to read, which programmes to watch, which football team to support, which toys to play with.

'The older you get the more decisions you can make for yourself, so that you get a choice to live your life as you want it. Being able to think things through and make wise decisions is a big asset to everyone. Can anyone give an example of someone they know making a decision that really helped them? What decisions have your parents made which affected you, for example, moving house, going on holiday?'

Agreements 1

'I would like you to return to your original groups of six now and discuss this issue. Imagine that you all have a birthday in the near future and your parents have offered you the choice of celebrating it by having a party in your own home or taking some friends out for a meal, perhaps to McDonald's or Pizza Hut. Everyone put forward their reasons for and against for both places. Then all have a turn at saying what her choice would be and why.'

Return to the whole group and ask for contributions. 'Was it an easy or hard decision? Did others think of reasons you had not thought of? Were you influenced by the decisions of others?' Emphasise the value of examining all the options before arriving at a decision.

Agreements 2

An alternative or additional activity would be to ask the children in groups of six to consider the games which are played in Circle Time and to choose the ones they like best, giving reasons. They could go on to discover the ingredients of a good game, for example, pleasure and enjoyment, fairness, co-operation and clear rules.

It is like making a cake, each part is important, they have to be mixed properly for something good to be made. Between them can they invent a game which they can demonstrate and then get the whole group to play?

Lighthouse

All hold hands and do a Lighthouse. Remind children that the light from a Lighthouse shines in order to help people. It shines in a friendly way, helping everyone that is near it. Ask everyone to look around the circle, make eye contact with some, and smile. This should be a quick activity and done silently. It stops when the hands are parted, which the teacher initiates.

Plan for the day

At the end of each Circle Time (if it's done at the beginning of the day) before anyone gets up, take the opportunity to announce what the plan for the rest of the day will be, to involve the children in the organisation, to remind them of equipment needed and where to find it, to tell them where they need to be at particular times, for example, appointments for doctors or swimming lessons. Wish everyone a happy and productive day. Do the children have any questions or comments?

Circle Time to promote a sense of competence 4

 ### Opening round

'Something I have done well recently is … .'

 ### Selection of child

 ### Instructions

Demonstrate, by asking the children to give you detailed instructions, how to water a plant. Have all equipment ready. Obey their instructions literally or without thinking, for example, if asked to get water – get it in your hand, or take a jug and hold it by the spout. The children will soon get the hang of it. Have some other simple task ready and get them to instruct each other so they learn how important it is to be precise.

 ### Accuracy

As an alternative, ask the children to mime something they enjoy doing or can do well. Begin by telling the children a story, if possible of a particular incident personal to yourself. Tell the story twice. In the first version blame everything that happens to you on someone and everything around you. In the second one own responsibility for everything that happens. An example would be an elaboration of a story about a minor traffic incident:

'I was driving to school at the correct speed and making sure I was aware of all the other vehicles and pedestrians in the road. As I approached a junction I saw some children making a nuisance of themselves on the pavement. Then, without warning, a car came out of a side road and hit me. It was completely his fault.'

And version two:

'I was in a hurry to get to school as I was late getting up and still feeling tired. There were some children on the pavement waving to some others so my attention was distracted and I did not see the car coming out of the side road in front of me, so we collided. I was not able to stop in time.' Ask the children to identify the differences. Ask who it is that really gets harmed when we choose to ignore taking the responsibility. Is there ever a valid reason for not telling a story accurately?

Either in small groups or the whole group, encourage the children to share experiences of this kind, if possible, giving two accounts of the same incident in the way described.

Tell them that it is often easier to blame others than it is to take responsibility ourselves when something is not right. Point out that it is always possible to change our own actions, but not necessarily those of others.

 ### Reports

Get the children to make some kind of self-assessment frequently. Ask them who is ultimately responsible for their learning? What is the teacher's function? An opportunity to record their comments in a book devoted to the purpose, suitably embellished with their own artwork, might be welcomed. If this is agreed with the children, parents can learn a lot about the children from them.

Examples:

This week/year I am pleased with the way I have ...

I have enjoyed ...

I have not enjoyed ...

Next week/year I shall ... differently.

Lighthouse

All hold hands and do a Lighthouse. Remind children that the light from a Lighthouse shines in order to help people. It shines in a friendly way, helping everyone that is near it. Ask everyone to look around the circle, make eye contact with some, and smile. This should be a quick activity and done silently. It stops when the hands are parted, which the teacher initiates.

Plan for the day

At the end of each Circle Time (if it's done at the beginning of the day) before anyone gets up, take the opportunity to announce what the plan for the rest of the day will be, to involve the children in the organisation, to remind them of equipment needed and where to find it, to tell them where they need to be at particular times, for example, appointments for doctors or swimming lessons. Wish everyone a happy and productive day. Do the children have any questions or comments?

This
Winner's Certificate
has been awarded to

for

Congratulations!
Well done!
It is good to feel
proud.

Circle Time to promote a sense of competence 5

 ### Circle whisper

Start the day by holding hands and sending a positive message round the circle. The leader whispers the message into the ear of the child on the right or left, who passes it on to the next person in a similar fashion, and so on, until the person who sent the message receives it herself. 'Have a good day', 'Be happy', 'Try something new today', are examples. Let the children initiate the message. Remind them that it should be something they want to hear themselves.

 ### Round

'I'm ... [name] and I am proud that I ... .'

 ### Back-writing

In pairs ask the children to use their fingers to write a word or phrase on their partner's back. Demonstrate first. Ask them to make only positive statements, for example 'To the top', 'Go for it', 'I like you'. The recipients can either say what the words are or have paper and pencil ready to write them down and then ask their partners to confirm if they are correct. Variations include writing on the palm of the hand or forehead with the recipient's eyes closed.

 ### Having a laugh

'Choose two partners who are making the funniest face and sit closely together so you can talk. Decide in which order you will speak. Tell each other about either the funniest time or the most enjoyable time you can remember.'

Good times

In the whole group ask them to recall any of their partner's funny experiences (with permission, of course). 'What makes people laugh or smile? What different kinds of laughter are there? Who will demonstrate? Are there any volunteers to try to make us laugh? You can tell a joke, clown about or just by laughing see if you can get us to join in.' At the end ask if smiling and laughing helps people to do their work better and to get on well with others. Is it a useful characteristic to be able to get people to laugh and smile?

'Knock, knock.'	Who's there?'
'Doctor'.	'Doctor Who?'
'I have a pig with no nose.'	'How does it smell?'
'Terrible'.	

Circle wave

Each child has a turn to give a wave to someone else in the circle. Then everyone waves together – as if they have just seen a friend they have not seen for a long time, perhaps at the airport reception area. This can all be done silently or when everyone is waving saying 'Hello' and 'How are you?' can be allowed to get to a really friendly crescendo!

Rounds

'Today/this week/this weekend/this holiday I am looking forward to … .'

'Today/this week/this weekend/this holiday I wish everyone … .'

Lighthouse

All hold hands and do a Lighthouse. Remind children that the light from a Lighthouse shines in order to help people. It shines in a friendly way, helping everyone that is near it. Ask everyone to look around the circle, make eye contact with some, and smile. This should be a quick activity and done silently. It stops when the hands are parted, which the teacher initiates.

Plan for the day

At the end of each Circle Time (if it's done at the beginning of the day) before anyone gets up, take the opportunity to announce what the plan for the rest of the day will be, to involve the children in the organisation, to remind them of equipment needed and where to find it, to tell them where they need to be at particular times, for example, appointments for doctors or swimming lessons. Wish everyone a happy and productive day. Do the children have any questions or comments?

Follow-up

Badge: Competence badge. Yes I can.

Circles to Promote a Sense of Well-Being

Activities for use anytime

We all need a hug in the morning
And one at the end of the day
With as many as possible squeezed in between,
The hug is the best cure of all.

Irish song

Activities for use anytime

These activities, properly presented, really will promote a sense of well-being. They are to be included in any Circle Time, but if time is limited, pick one and do it on its own. Like most of the other circle activities they can all be used with any age group – use them frequently. The three visualisation exercises, The Quick Relax, The Magic Island, My Best Friend, are abbreviated versions of ones that can be found on the CD. They are printed here as you may wish to present them to the group yourself and so time the pauses to suit, but if the group is new to guided imagery, bear in mind that the CD starts by giving the reasons for doing this activity and the next two sections are practices for what is to come. In My Best Friend there is a reference to the school gate, which you will need to change if this is not appropriate to fit the situation you are in. An explanation of the self-esteem value of these visualisations and the best way to use them is given in Chapter 9.

Gratitude activities

Many benefits of the power of giving thanks have been listed in gratitude research, including higher levels of positive emotions, vitality and life satisfaction and less depression and stress. In experiments, higher levels of goal achievement were witnessed, as was a greater willingness to help others.

A   Collecting gratitudes. In triads each child names something or a quality she is grateful for. It can be big or small, important or not important. Share the reasons. Make a list. Draw pictures.

B   Circle gratitudes. Each person in the circle names a gratitude and is thanked by the group either collectively or individually. 'Name. Thank you for telling us that'.

C   Pats on the back. Each person writes a letter to parent, teacher, friend, anyone who deserves a thank you.

D   Gratitude diary. Each day record things you are grateful for. Focus on each one in turn and allow and encourage the feeling of appreciation that arises.

> Gratitude is not only the greatest of virtues,
> but the parent of all the others.
>
> Cicero

Walking therapy

Move any furniture and create the largest possible space in the middle of the room.

'Please stand in a space as far away from anyone else as is possible. I am going to ask you to do some walking now. There are going to be four different ways to do it. I will describe the first one and then ask you to do it just for a minute or two. Then I will stop you, describe the next and so on. The first way is this:

'I would like you to fold your arms and look down. When I say "Go" start moving but make sure you do not bump into anyone. Just keep your head down and avert your eyes. Give everyone a wide berth. Any questions? All right. Go.'

(The time should be short, but long enough for you to judge that people are uncomfortable moving like this.)

'Stop please. You can unfold your arms now and look up. I again want you to take a walk around the room but this time relax your arms and look about you, but if you make eye contact avoid any sign of recognition. Any questions? All right. Go.'

(Again judge the length of time to see that people are reacting.)

'Stop please. Number three. Something totally different. Start thinking of nice things to say to people. This time move around the room and go up to people, greet them, and exchange a compliment. Time will be given for you to meet at least three people. You won't have time to get into a conversation. Just stop, greet, consider and give a compliment. It can be about anything at at all, appearance, behaviour, attendance, etc. Acknowledge the compliment that you receive, of course.'

(The number of people to greet depends on how many in the group. If it's large, increase to give time to get around the room, observe reactions.) 'Stop please. Just one more walkabout. This time again approach people, greet them but then tell them something good about yourself, a quality you have which you like, something you have done, share something you feel proud of. Your partner will acknowledge your strength, pleasure or achievement with 'It sounds as if', or similar. Again three people please, but you will have a bit more time to be with your partners this time so no rush when talking about yourself. Any questions? OK. Start please.'

(If group is large give time to meet more people, but not too long. Judge and observe reactions.)

'Stop please. Now – when I say "Go" – you will approach two people who you have spoken to in the course of your walkabout and ask them to join you as a group, a triad, and find somewhere comfortable to sit. When I see everyone is in place I will let you know what to do next. Go.' (Give time for groups to form and be seated.)

'Everyone, I would now like you to do some rounds. Take it in turns to finish these sentence stems. There are four and I will tell you them all now so there is no waiting. When you have done the rounds I expect you will want to say more to each other about the experience you have just had and how it relates to your life, so I am going to leave some time for you to do that and will give you two minutes' notice when it is time to stop. Each person takes a turn to finish the first stem then goes on to the next.

'The stems are, in order:

When I did the first walk with arms folded and looking down I felt ...

When I did the second walk but still had to avoid people I felt ...

When I did the third walk and gave people compliments I felt ...

When I did the fourth walk and told people something positive about myself I felt ...

'Any questions? Then everyone start.'

(Judge time needed and then bring everyone back into a circle and ask for sharing.)

Moan time

'I get upset by ... .'

'I hate it when ... .'

Use these rounds to give the opportunity for children to say what is troubling them, whether it is caused by anger, fear, frustration, or disappointment. Encouraging the expression of these feelings is healthy; children learn that everyone has them and that they don't have to be ashamed of them or repress them. We first have to recognise what's happening inside, then we can deal with it.

If any difficulties that are aired can be resolved in the group so much the better, but set limits on exploring strategies to do so. The prime purpose of the activity is to acknowledge feelings. Listen empathetically and validate the speaker's feelings. Help to find words which label the emotion accurately. Support the speaker with remarks such as 'It sounds as if that is really unpleasant/worrying/annoying to you', and leave it at that.

✝✝✝ Circle support

Ask how we can give strength to others. Often we touch them and have feelings of support for them.

'All join hands and close eyes. Gently but firmly take the hands of those on either side of you. Imagine that everyone in the circle needs your help and support. Sit quietly for a moment and through your hands send your help and support to everyone'. (Pause.) 'Now think of everyone sending their support to you. See if you can find a good feeling inside which comes from being here with everyone else.'

> A noble person is mindful and thankful of the favours
> he receives from others
>
> the Buddha

Deep breathing

'Sit upright or kneel and put your hands, palm downwards, on your stomach so that the tips of the fingers are just touching each other. Begin to breathe slowly and deeply, in and out, and as you do so, feel your fingers separating and coming together. Close your eyes, maintain a steady rhythm and enjoy the peaceful feeling that comes with it.'

Listening

Repeat breathing exercise, then invite children to sit or lie quietly and comfortably on the floor.

'This activity is about listening, really using your ears. You will find you can do this better if you close your eyes. First I would like you to see if you can identify any sounds you can hear that are coming from outside the building. Can you hear people or vehicles or machines or animals or birds? Listen to them for a moment.' (Pause.)

'Now can you hear any sounds or noises being made inside the building – telephones, people moving about, doors opening or closing? Listen to them'. (Pause.)

'Now listen to sounds being made in this room. Can you hear anyone moving or breathing? Anything apart from my voice?' (Pause.)

'Last I would like you to try to cut out all the other sounds and spend a short time just listening to the sounds inside yourself – the quiet, steady breathing we can all do. Just enjoy listening to your breathing.' (Pause.) 'When you are ready I would like you to open your eyes, sit up, have a good stretch, look around the room, and then come back into the circle.' Discuss how we can choose what to hear, and how much we can miss because of the way we are. Ask the children if and when they experience silence and what their feelings are about it. Mention different lifestyle options – in the city, in the country, living in a crowd, living alone. We all have a choice.

The Quick Relax

Step one: 'Be aware if you are upset (for example, have a pain, headache, sweaty palms, fast heart beat, etc.).'

Step two: 'Smile inwardly and tell yourself to become calm.'

Step three: 'Now I would like you to imagine that the surface of your feet is covered with tiny, magic holes.' (The children may giggle at this but the image appeals to them.) 'They are usually covered by shutters but you can open them with your mind at any time.

'Do that now and then, breathing slowly and easily, think of cool air flowing through the holes, up through your legs into your stomach. Hold the air like that for a second and then let it go back down your body and legs, out through the holes, taking all your tensions and worries with it. Do that several times at your own speed.'

Step four: 'Go in your mind to that place where you are fully relaxed and happy wherever that particular place is – perhaps a bed, someone's lap, playing with a pet, on a bicycle. Imagine all the details:

What are you wearing? Who is with you?

What can you hear, smell, touch?

What are you feeling inside now?

Ask children to think of times in the past when it would have been helpful to know how to relax quickly. Is it a useful thing to do on occasions? Where in their bodies do they feel the tension? (Each of us usually has a favourite place!) Remind them of the power of self-talk and the phrase 'No matter what you say or do to me I am still a worthwhile person'. Some children enjoy doing longer relaxation exercises and being introduced to yoga. Children are now being shown how to massage each other which is a good idea.

> All the things I got in trouble for dreaming those days in school I am doing today. And I cannot encourage that enough for any children or any people who want to do anything in life. If you visualise and be clear enough in living colour it is going to happen. As long as you are willing to work for it, it is going to happen. I really believe that. And that is what happened to me.
>
> Michael Flatley, 'Lord of the Dance',
> television documentary, October 1997

Floating Thoughts

'Please find a space and get yourselves comfortable. Either sit upright or lie down on your backs. Today we are going to use our imaginations, that part of the mind that sees pictures and can create anything we wish. Before we start, slowly and quietly take some deep breaths. Inhale, hold the breath for a moment, then slowly release it. Feel your body becoming relaxed and comfortable, the floor supporting you. And as your body becomes still, your mind becomes open and alert. So close your eyes please. I would like you now to think of a nice quiet place that you know. It can be where you have been or perhaps you have seen a picture of it. It's got to be a place in the open so it can be a garden, a park, a field, the beach. You will think of somewhere and, when you do, put yourself in the picture. You are by yourself and you look around and take in your surroundings. Everything looks good and you are pleased to be there.' Pause.

'You are sitting there and having a think. Recently something has happened which caused you to have a feeling that was not pleasant. Did you get cross, sad, worried, anxious? Something upset you and before you knew it this feeling was there. Feel it inside you again now – just for a moment.' Pause.

'Got it? Well, I have a surprise for you. Right next to you you can see a balloon. Pick it up and prepare to blow it up. Hold it and then off you go. Put your lips together and as you blow you will find that the feeling you were having is going – and where do you think it is going? Into the balloon of course. Blow all of it in and tie it up. Maybe the balloon has changed colour, gone dark, black. Then you know that the feeling is there. Along comes the wind, so let it go and watch as it goes up and away, higher and further until it goes out of sight. It looked like a dark cloud and now it's gone. That's great.

'Do you feel a change? Strong perhaps, lighter, warmer. The sun comes out, maybe birds are singing, other creatures moving about, butterflies, dogs or a cat, maybe some people start coming into the picture. Someone is flying a kite, perhaps. You certainly feel more relaxed so you slowly get up and go for a gentle stroll, looking at everything, seeing people smile at you and you smile back. And just when you are ready, let that nice walk lead you right back into the group here in the room. And again, when you are ready, open your eyes, have a good stretch and then join us in the circle.

The Magic Island

Ask the children to find a space and to either sit upright or lie down on their backs.

'Today we are going to use our imaginations, that part of the mind that sees pictures and can create anything we wish. Before we start, slowly and quietly take some deep breaths. Inhale, hold the breath for a moment, then slowly release it. Feel your body becoming relaxed and comfortable, the floor supporting you. And as your body becomes still, your mind becomes open and alert. Now I would ask you to let your imagination take you to a small island. It's got fields, trees, streams, a river, a beach, and the sea. It's a lovely place, somewhere you like to be. The sun is shining and warm, the wind is blowing gently, the birds are singing. You can decide just where you want to go, do what you want to do.

Think of one thing you would like to do, walk in the woods, climb to the top of a tree, sit in a field, lie on the beach, paddle in the sea. You decide and then do it'. (Pause.)

'Really enjoy doing it. Feel the grass or the sand or the water, whatever it is. Do what you like without hurrying, no one is going to tell you to do something different. Is there anything to hear where you are? ... anything to smell? ... anything to touch? What is the best thing about being where you are – on your island? This is a special place you have found. Really enjoy being there and how wonderful it is.' (Pause.)

'Remember, this is a place you can return to at any time. Now, in your own time, when you are ready, I would like you to come back to the classroom. Have a slow stretch, open your eyes, sit up and return to the circle.

My Best Friend

'I would like you to find a space and get as comfortable as you can. So that you can really relax and enjoy this, take some deep breaths, very quietly so no one else can hear. Draw the breath in, hold it and then slowly release it. Do this several times. Check your body, your arms and legs, everywhere, to see if you can feel any tension. If you can, send some relaxing breath to that place. When you are ready, close your eyes and start to enjoy the feeling of going on a journey in your imagination. It starts with you in a field. The grass is just as you like it, there are some flowers growing in it and perhaps some little creatures scurrying around going about their business. You are enjoying being there, the sun is shining and everything is fine. You can see a path which leads into some woods so you decide to walk along it. You cross the field and walk into the woods, perhaps kicking up the leaves as you go or looking out for rabbits or squirrels. As you go further you realise that the wood is at the bottom of a mountain. You decide to climb it and you are soon on an open path going upwards. It gets quite steep, but that doesn't stop you. You have plenty of energy and now you are determined to reach the top. There are easy parts, there are rocky places. Your legs are working hard, you breathe deeply and feel strong. You go on and on, up and up, until finally at last you are there. You find that it is a really beautiful place and you are pleased to have reached it ...'. (Pause.)

'Sitting there already you see a child who waves and smiles at you. You both move to meet and greet each other. Soon you are talking and playing together as if you have been friends for a long time. You know that this person is special to you and will always be your friend. You know you can talk about anything with your friend and you will always get help and support and good company. If there are any questions you want to ask, you will always get a good answer ...'. (Pause.)

'You can always trust this person to know what is best for you ...'. (Pause.) 'You really enjoy being with your friend and doing the things you both like doing. You have more fun than you've ever had ...'. (Pause.) Now it's time to leave. Your friend says you can come back at any time and you say you will visit often. You say good-bye and go back down the path and through the woods feeling very pleased to have met your friend and to know you can return whenever you want.

'The path leads you through the field and comes to the school gate. You walk through and into the school and into this room. Have a stretch and yawn. Open your eyes gently and when you are ready come back into the circle.'

Then allow the children time to draw or write about their experience. The paper and materials should have been given out before the visualisation so that they can begin immediately without interruption. Follow up with a discussion with volunteers showing their drawings and talking about them. If time is limited have the discussion only. See the next chapter for more details.

Picture This: Guided Imagery for Everyone

Guidance on how to use the CD and explanations of the self-esteem concepts projected in each of the visualisations on it

> The human mind is not, as philosophers would have you think, a debating hall, but a picture gallery.
>
> D.E. Harding, philosopher

Each section deals with an aspect of self-esteem. Use the exercises often. Their value should not be judged by doing them only once. The more frequently they are done the more the listeners become accustomed to them and benefit from them.

 ## Guided imagery

One of the most powerful ways to help children and teenagers build their self-esteem is to give them an early introduction to guided imagery. There are many benefits for adults too – the development of the imagination and intuition, improved concentration and memory skills, a better ability to deal with stress and in consequence a real sense of well-being, are some of the advantages which can accrue through imagery work. It will help to increase internal motivation and to raise academic achievement. It can lead to more self-confidence, greater self-respect, and be an important factor in having a really healthy level of self-esteem.

Children enjoy the experience as it is certain they will already have used their imaginations to take them to the world of make believe using their toys and teddies and finding imaginary friends who are very real to them. When they are told a bedtime story they will snuggle under the duvet and happily see in their mind's eye pictures of the characters and their adventures. Later, at school, told to sit up and pay attention, a pupil will stop drifting with Cleopatra on her golden throne somewhere on the Nile and listen again to the teacher's version of Antony and Cleopatra. Our imaginations are at work all the time everywhere.

> Children with imaginary companions have more advanced communication skills.
>
> Ann Rob, psychologist, Manchester University

We need to acknowledge the importance of our imagination and be aware of what a powerful tool for good it can be in our lives. We should remember that every man-made object that we see and use is the product of someone's imagination. Think of chairs, for example, how many thousands and thousands of different designs of chairs there are in existence yet every single one started life as a picture in someone's head. From cottages to castles, from canoes to battleships, someone had to think of what it would look like first. It's an inspiring thought.

Just as we can use our imagination to create wonderful, awe-inspiring objects, so we can use it to enhance the quality of our lives in a different way – by building, strengthening and maintaining our self-esteem. By listening to and meditating on the stories told here, internal messages will be received which will reinforce all those positive qualities we all possess and which we need to help us on our journey through life. Once aware of the possibilities of enhancing self-esteem using this strategy I am sure readers will want to think of other stories for themselves that will have a similar effect.

If you are a parent, teacher or carer of children or teenagers in any capacity I hope you will make time to listen to this CD, together with them, in a quiet, comfortable place and that everyone will enjoy and benefit from the experience.

How to use the Picture This

Please read these notes and listen to the exercises before using the CD with young people. No prior knowledge of imagery work is needed to use it. It is designed to gently introduce the listeners to cultivating their imaginations and contains clear instructions. Each section is self-contained and has an explanation of its purpose.

The exercises were originally devised to use in schools during Circle Times but they are equally suitable for use in any situation where visualistion work is included. Although most of them contain reference to the group they can also be used by individuals with advantage.

The CD has been used successfully in reception classes, in junior and secondary schools, youth clubs and also adult groups. Parents have obtained it for use by the family.

Pauses between tracks

There are pauses left on the tracks in order for the participants to focus on their own imagery. In order to include as much material as possible on the one disc most of the pauses that come in the exercises are very short. It was considered that the amount of time required for the participants to focus on their imagery must vary with the age and other variables of the group. In consultation with the participants, the length of the pauses is best left to the judgement of the teacher or group leader who can then use the appropriate button on the recorder. The alternative is to let the CD run as it stands without intervention. Children who listen to it by themselves can happily be left to do this without loss of the values of the exercise. Good quality sound reproduction is vital.

When I examine myself and my methods of thought I come to the conclusion that the gift of fantasy has meant more to me than my talent for absorbing positive knowledge.

Albert Einstein 1875–1955, scientist and philosopher

The stories in the tracks

I do recommend that everyone listens to the first three tracks initially. Beginning with an explanation of the purpose of guided imagery and the benefits to be gained from it, the tracks offer a variety of experiences of it. The listeners are first introduced to visualising people and places in school and at home and then learn that imagery involves an awareness of all the senses. Next, this valuable process is used to show how both body and mind can be calm and relaxed, while the last two tracks lead the listener to pictures of events and places where they will feel safe and secure.

The second track refers to being in a classroom and if this is not appropriate to your situation will need an explanation and substitution before listening to it. The last four tracks are visualisations and should preferably be used in the order they are given. Each one leads listeners on journeys where different aspects of self-esteem are built and when put together offer a firm foundation for growth.

Location

When listening to the CD always choose a comfortable environment, free from distractions as much as possible. Turn off phones and try to prevent interruptions. The position to be used for listening has to be a personal choice. Sitting on a chair, sitting cross legged on the floor, or lying down. I believe people get the best images when in a horizontal position. Do make sure there is plenty of space between people and be prepared for the child who is restless and not absorbed in the imagery.

Closing eyes

Some may not feel safe enough to close their eyes so this cannot be mandatory. However, a good reason to do so is given in section 2 and with the leader's encouragement, hopefully all will soon be persuaded to do it. You may like to explain that it is easier to use the imagination when you reduce other outputs to the brain. When children and young people are listening it is strongly recommended that no observers are there to watch this activity. Only the teacher/leader needs to do this. Any other adults must be required to take a full part and they can then match their reactions to those of the children.

Reflections

Only ever listen to one track at a time and always allow time at the end to discuss what was heard and what reactions people had to it. People will usually like to say what they saw and the adventures they had. Certainly the children will. After listening to any of the tracks 7–10 encourage everyone to reflect on the experience.

Did the pictures that they saw and the things that they did in the imagery have any special significance for them?

What are their reactions to the journey?

Do they have any questions about it?

Do they need to ask you to explain something?

Make sure that you share too. Take the lead when necessary.

Sometimes prompts for completion can be helpful:

The imagery made me feel ...

The imagery made me remember ...

The most powerful image that I had ...

Drawing

If time allows it is especially beneficial to have drawings done first which then form the basis for the ensuing discussion. It is essential that paper and drawing materials are immediately to hand, so distribute some before the exercise begins, otherwise there is a break in the continuity and thoughts and emotions are lost. Ask the participants to draw what they saw or felt. Explain that this is free expression, so symbols, squiggles, patterns, any free expression and quick drawings are all acceptable. Only a few minutes are needed, with 30 seconds' notice of time to finish being given. The discussion, which of course is best done in a circle, starts with a volunteer showing what has been drawn and saying what it represents. No one is coerced into showing their picture, or taking part generally, but if the right climate has been established this will not present a problem.

More than once

Just one track at a time is used for a session, but do not listen to it only once. The more frequently they are used the easier it is to witness the positive changes guided imagery can bring about. Most of the sections will bear lots of repeats. Often new pictures, ideas and a deeper understanding are revealed to the listener on a second or subsequent listening. Imagery work can be a powerful tool for helping with hypersensitivity or troublesome behaviour and all kinds of difficulties presented by children and teenagers with low self-esteem.

> Imaginary friends? It is a normal phenomenon for normal children and it is very healthy. Imaginary friends often stay with them through the teenage years providing comfort and escape – although in secret.
>
> Karen Majors, educational psychologist, Institute of Education, London

Try some yourself

The discussions that arise from these exercises can provide exciting incentives for the promoton of literacy in the classsroom. Apart from talking about their own reactions to the suggested imagery children may like to consider the purpose and value of this approach. Speaking and listening are an essential part of the Framework and using this material can contribute to its development in an innovative way. The pupils could also be asked to devise some exercises of their own, either on CD or paper, and try them on the rest of the class.

> If I am in a situation I don't like but can't change
> Then I remember I can change my attitude to it
>
> Brian Patten b. 1946, English poet

The tracks

Side A

1 Introduction	**3:28 mins**

This section explains in a very simple way what guided imagery is about and the benefits that can come from practising it.

2 Practice: The Classroom	**5:04 mins**

Perhaps a first conscious experience of using the imagination.

Remaining in the same room, but picturing other members of class doing something different from the usual.

3 Practice: My Home   3:18 mins

Seeing a familiar place without actually being there.

Realising that the imagination employs all the senses –
sound, smell, taste, touch, as well as sight.

4 Relax and Feel Good   4:57 mins

Learning a practical way to use the mind in order to remain calm
and relaxed. Discovering that movement helps the process.

5 The Quick Relax   4:49 mins

A very helpful technique to have handy when upset about something.
A fast, fun way to combat stress which appeals to children of all ages.
Good to practise so it can be instantly recalled when needed.

6 The Place To Be   8:00 mins

Relaxing first with toy soldiers and floppy dolls, we go on a
journey looking at leaves floating away on a river and watching
snowflakes falling to the ground before we finally arrive at a
place we really like to be.

Side B

7 The Magic Island   4:53 mins

To enjoy being on this lovely island we see that we have choices to
consider and a decision to make. We learn that using our imaginations
to return here briefly before we have to make real life decisions may be
an asset. We can become aware that we are thinking for ourselves and
not being swayed by peer pressure and the need to conform.

8 My Best Friend   **7:18 mins**

The message here is that we are the most powerful people in our lives and that self-confidence and self-repect is a gift we give to ourselves. The victim never need feel lonely if s/he remembers there is always someone at the top of the mountain. Our best friend will always be there for us no matter what happens.

9 The Road To Success   **5:28 mins**

Encouraging goal-setting and achieving targets fosters a sense of purpose, a key element of self-esteem. Fulfilling any ambition involves risk, and success depends on planning wisely and never hesitating to ask for help.

10 Dancing On A Rainbow   **8:53 mins**

Life can be a journey of adventure and fun. Self-esteem gives us the confidence to discover and enjoy that which is new wherever we look for it. Where better to find it than in ourselves. We all possess the potential to be everything we want to be.

References and Resources

Prelims

Coopersmith, S. (1981) *The Antecedents of Self-Esteem.* Palo Alto, CA: Consulting Psychologists Press.
Dahl, R. (2001) *The Minpins.* London: Puffin.
de Saint Exupéry, A. (1943) *Le Petit Prince.* Gallimard. Various English translations in print.
Osho (1998) *Beyond Pshchology.* Cologne: Rebel House Publishing.

Chapter 1: Self-Esteem

Branden, N. (1969) *The Psychology of Self-Esteem.* San Fransisco, CA: Jossey-Bass.
Branden, N. (1982) *The Power Of Self-Esteem.* Deerfield Beach, FL: Health Communications.
Branden, N. (1998) *How To Raise Your Self-Esteem.* New York: Bantam.
Branden, N. (1994) *The Art of Living Consciously.* San Francisco, CA: Jossey-Bass.
Branden, N. (2004) *The Six Pillars of Self-Esteem.* New York: Random House.
California Task Force (1990) *Towards a State of Esteem.* California: California State Department.
Gerhardt, S. (2004) *Why Love Matters. How Affection Shapes a Baby's Brain.* Brunner-Routledge.
Gilmore, John V. (1971) 'The Productive Personality'. *Journal of Education,* 154, 1, 5–39.
Health Education Authority (1996) now part of NICE – Natonal institute for Health and Clinical Excellence
Kernis, M.H. (ed.) (2006) *Self-Esteem: Issues and Answers.* New York: Psychology Press.
Maslow, A. (1968) *Toward a Psychology of Being.* New York: Van Nostrand Reinhold.
Mecca, A., Smelser, N., and Vasconcellos, J. (1989) *The Social Importance of Self-Esteem.* Berkeley, CA: University of California Press.
Mruk, C. (199) *Self-Esteem: Research, Theory and Practice,* second edition. Free Association Books.
Shindler, J.V. *Creating a Psychology of Success in the Classroom.* Los Angeles: California State University.
The Primary Review (2007) *Community Surroundings* – Interim Report of the Primary Review, a Cambridge University project.

Chapter 2: Your Self-Esteem

Brown, J. (1986) *I only Want What's Best for You.* New York: Saint Martin's Press.
Carlson, R. (1997) *Stop Thinking and Start Living.* Hammersmith: Thorsons.
Duncan, J. (1997) *Change Your Thoughts – Change Your Life.* Living Well.
Ferrucci, P. (1982) *What We May Be.* Winnipeg, Canada: Turnstone Press.
Gawain, S. (1985) *Creative Visualisation.* New York: Bantam.
Glouberman, D. (1989) *Life Choices Life Changes Through Imagework.* San Rafael, CA: Mandala.
Holden, R. (2000) *Shift Happens.* Hodder & Stoughton.
Johnson, S. and Blanchard, K. (1982) *The One Minute Manager.* New Jersey: William Morrow & Co.
Robbins, A. (2000) *Awaken the Giant Within.* Pocket Books.
Scott Peck, M. (1990) *The Road Less Travelled.* Arrow Books.
Shine, B. (1991) *Mind Magic.* Corgi Books.
Watts, A. (1971) *Psychotherapy East and West.* London: Argus & Robertson.

Chapter 3: Leading a group

Bolton, R. (1986) *People Skills.* New Jersey: Prentice Hall.
Heron, J. (1993) *Group Facilitation.* London: Kogan Page.
Heron, J. (1989) *The Facilitator's Handbook.* London: Kogan Page.
Rogers, C. (2004) *On Becoming A Person.* London: Constable.

Chapters 4, 5, 6: Circle Time links

Berne, E. (1996) *Games People Play.* New York: Grove Press.

Brady, P.J., Figuerres, C.I., Felker, D.W., and Garrison, W.M. (2006) 'Predicting Student Self-Concept, Anxiety and Responsibility from Self-Evaluation and Self-Praise'. *Psychology in the Schools,*15, 3 434–8.

Briggs, Dorothy C. (1970) *Your Child's Self-Esteem.* New York: Doubleday.

Cartwright-Hatton, S. (2006) 'Anxiety in a Neglected Population: Prevalence of an Anxiety Disorder in Pre-Adolescent Children'. *Clinical Psychology Review, 26,* 817–33.

Friere, P. (2006) *Teachers as Cultural Workers: Letters to those who Desire to Teach.* Boulder, CO: Westviewpress.

Cousins, N. (1979) *Anatomy of an Illness.* New York: W.W.Norton.

Ginott, H. (1995) *Teacher and Child.* New York: Collier.

Goldman, D. (1996) *Emotional Intelligence. Why It Can Matter More Than IQ.* London: Bloomsbury.

Keating, K. (1986) *The Little Book of Hugs.* London: Angus & Robertson.

Mortimer, P., Sammons, P., Stoll, L., Lewis, D. and Ecob, R. (1988) *School Matters, The Junior Years.* Open Book Publishing.

Neill, A.S. (1970) *Summerhill, A Radical Approach to Education.* Harmondsworth: Pelican.

Purkey, W. (1970) *Self-Concept and School Achievement.* New Jersey: Prentice Hall.

Robins, L.N. and Rutter, M. (1992) *Straight and Devious Pathways from Childhood to Adulthood.* Cambridge: Cambridge University Press.

Senge, P. (2000) *Schools That Learn.* New York: Doubleday.

Seligman, M. (2002) *Authentic Happiness.* New York: Free Press.

Steiner, C. (2002) *Emotional Literacy. Intelligence With A Heart.* Fawnskin, CA: Personhood Press.

Whitty, G. and Wisbey, E. (2007) *Real Decision Making: Schools Councils in Action.* Institute of Education, University of London.

Chapter 7: Circle Times for All

Assagioli, R. (1971) *Psycosynthesis.* London: Penguin.

Byers, Betsy (1973) *The 18th Emergency.* Several publishers, in print since 1973.

Emmons, R.A. and McCollough, M.E. (2004) *The Psychology of Gratitude.* New York: Oxford University Press.

Gottman, J. (1997) *The Heart of Parenting.* London: Bloomsbury.

Health Education Authority (1996) now part of NICE – National Insitute for Health and Clinical Excellence.

Heide, Florence Parry (1992) *The Shrinking of Treehorn.* New York: Harry Abrams.

Jaffe, A. (1978) 'Symbolism in the Visual Arts' in *Man and his Symbols* ed. Cart Jung. London: Picador.

James, M. and Jongward, D. (1971) *Born to Win.* Menlo Park, CA: Addison-Wesley.

Miller, A. (1990) *The Untouched Key.* London: Virago.

Murduck, M. (1987) *Spinning Inward, Using Guided Imagery with Children for Learning Creativity and Relaxation.* Boston, MA: Shambala.

Raspe, R.E. (1895) *The Surprising Adventures of Baron Munchausen.* Several publishers.

Senge, P. (1990) *The Fith Discipline.* New Yourk: Trasworld.

Simon, S. (1073) *IALAC – I Am Lovable And Capable.* Argus Communications.

Steiner, C. (1977) *The Warm Fuzzy Tale.* Fawnskin, CA: Jalmar Press.

The Primary Review (2007) *Community Soundings* – Interim Report of the Primary Review, a Cambridge University Project.

White, D. (2000) *Philosophy For Kids: 40 Fun Questions.* Austin, TX: Prufrock Press.

White, M. (2001) *50 Activities to Raise Self-Esteem.* Cambridge: Pearson Publishing.

White, M. *Circle Time DVD* (see www.murraywhite-circle time.co.uk)

Whitfield, P. (2006) *Zen Tails.* Frenchs Forest, Australia: New Frontier Publishing.

Williams, M. (1922) *The Velveteen Rabbit: How Toys Become Real.* Several publishers.